Encouraging
Classroom Success

Encouraging Classroom Success

Mel Ainscow
Tutor (Special Educational Needs), Cambridge Institute of Education

David A. Tweddle
General Adviser (Special Needs), Oldham

David Fulton Publishers
London

David Fulton Publishers Ltd
14 Chalton Drive London N2 0QW

First published in Great Britain by
David Fulton Publishers 1988

British Library Cataloguing in Publication Data

Ainscow, Mel
　　Encouraging classroom success.
　　1. Learning disordered children. Teaching
　　I. Title　　II. Tweddle, David A.
　　371.9′043

　　ISBN 1-85346-031-1

Typeset by Chapterhouse, Formby
Printed and bound in Great Britain by
St Edmundsbury Press

Contents

'The most important things that each man must learn, no one else can teach him.'

Sheldon Kopp

Preface

About two years ago we began work on a second edition of *Preventing Classroom Failure*, which was published in 1979. After a few months, so little remained of the original text that the attempt was abandoned. We decided, instead, to write a new book.

Encouraging Classroom Success is critical of a great deal of existing practice. We hope that our arguments do not cause offence, and ask readers who feel criticised to accept that probably the severest criticism contained in this book is self-criticism.

We have rejected the traditionally narrow perspective of remedial and special education in favour of an approach based on an assumption that *all* teaching should be made more effective. We offer a framework for evaluating the quality of teaching and learning that is applicable to teachers of *all* children and young people. It is rooted in the belief that the most important source of learning – for pupils *and* teachers – is personal experience.

We have resisted the temptation to pepper the text with examples and anecdotes. Whilst this has tended to be our style in previous publications, we feel that it would be inappropriate for a book of this kind. Similarly, the book is not cluttered with references; we acknowledge the work of others only when it would be unfair not to do so. However, a selection of useful sources is provided and described briefly at the end of each chapter.

Finally, we would warn readers not to expect cook-book solutions to 'special needs problems': *our aim is to help teachers find their own.*

Mel Ainscow and David A. Tweddle
February 1988

CHAPTER 1

Success in the Classroom

During the last twenty or thirty years, there has been a major growth in the range of provision and services for pupils with 'special educational needs' – whatever that term means. A great deal has changed over this period, not least the names we use to describe youngsters who are thought to have problems of one kind or another. The nature and style of the provision has also changed. In particular, recent years have seen an increased emphasis on providing services for such pupils within the ordinary class.

Despite increases in resources, changing fashions in terminology and the recent switch to supporting children in mainstream schools, one assumption has remained unchallenged. Whenever learning difficulties occur, it is assumed that there is a deficiency within the pupil. Learning difficulties are thought to be something which the pupil 'has'. As a result, we become preoccupied with an in-depth investigation of the child in an attempt to locate the 'fault'.

There is comfort and security in this assumption. As teachers, it will always let us off the hook! If there is something wrong with the pupil, it cannot possibly be our fault. What we teach, and the way we teach it, can continue as before. We can't lose.

We want to challenge this assumption. This does not necessarily imply assuming blame and guilt for each pupil's difficulties. The outcome can be much more positive and optimistic by switching the emphasis to factors over which we, as teachers, have influence. Instead of focusing on the pupil's limitations, let's concentrate on those things which we can do something about – *namely, our own teaching.*

Every day we make dozens of decisions in the classroom. By and large, *we* decide what's going to happen. These are the factors over which we have influence. This should be the focus of our attention. In this book we provide a framework for evaluating the quality of teaching and learning. It is intended to be applicable to teachers of *all* children and young people, and it is rooted in the assumption that the most important source of learning – for pupils and teachers – is personal experience.

Traditional approaches

The approaches that have been common to what was known as remedial and special education, but which is now more usually referred to as the field of special educational needs, have rightly emphasised the importance of considering pupils as individuals. Unfortunately this focus on individuality, linked as it often is with the assumption that learning difficulties occur mainly because of the limitations of particular pupils, has led us to adopt a narrow perspective. This narrowness has had a negative influence on the attitudes and practice of many teachers which, in turn, has been to the disadvantage of their pupils.

For example, the emphasis that has been placed on the need to identify particular pupils who have learning difficulties (or, more often these days, 'special needs') may have a significant effect on the expectations we have of what they can achieve. As a result, arrangements are made in order that they will not have to face experiences or challenges that are seen as being beyond them. This perceived need to protect 'special children' may be extended into the curriculum, which is then reduced to provide a diet that is felt to be more appropriate.

In addition, there is a tendency for teachers to doubt their own professional competence to deal with children who are 'special'. These children are felt to need special teaching, different methods of learning, and materials which have been designed to help them overcome their problems. Feelings of inadequacy may be reinforced by the presence of experts working with children who have special needs, who seem prepared to take responsibility for those pupils who create most anxiety for the teacher. Matters may be made even worse if the expert offers advice or special materials that seem so complex or time consuming that they cannot be used by a teacher who has to give attention to a full class.

An almost inevitable outcome of this focus on individual children is that they find themselves dealt with separately. This may mean that they are placed at least for part of the time in a separate class or group where they can be offered additional help, or they may be provided with separate tasks or materials to work with in the classroom. As a result they may spend long periods working in isolation from their fellow classmates, perhaps feeling somewhat rejected, and certainly gaining none of the potential educational and social benefits that can accrue from working closely with those who are more successful. It may also be the case that their tasks and activities are less challenging or even trivial in comparison with those in which the rest of the class are engaged.

The hidden message that is being given to the pupil as a result of what was intended as a form of positive discrimination is that he or she is inadequate and different. This often has a damaging effect on morale and confidence.

A more positive orientation

Recognising the potential dangers of this traditional approach to learning difficulties, we intend to adopt a radical view that is more optimistic, realistic and rational.

We believe that every adult and child, without exception, experiences learning difficulties in particular circumstances. Listening to, but failing to understand, a lecture; being able to complete less than half of the *Guardian* crossword; and becoming utterly confused as a result of reading a users' guide for a word processor, are all examples of learning difficulties experienced recently by the authors. Similarly, every reader will recall instances from the recent past, and possibly also from their childhood, when the presented task was apparently impossible.

If the tasks and activities in which the learner is engaged are not matched to the learner's existing capabilities, or are not understood by the learner, then learning difficulties are likely to occur. Thus, learning difficulties are context-specific and are, from time to time, experienced by everybody – teachers, pupils, parents and even writers of books about education.

We believe that this definition is:

○ **Realistic**
   It recognises the real problem faced by all teachers – that of teaching a large class of pupils who may all, occasionally at least, experience learning difficulties. It is not simply a case of providing some extra help for one or two.

○ **Rational**
   It does not automatically include or exclude academically

successful pupils, those for whom English is a second language, adolescents who seem difficult to motivate, or 'middle of the road' pupils who have no obvious strengths or weaknesses.

○ **Optimistic**
If learning difficulties are 'context-bound', in other words associated with particular tasks or circumstances, then they can be prevented or, indeed, created by teachers. Moreover, when they occur, as they inevitably will, they can be resolved.

This working definition of learning difficulties leads us to focus attention on the context within which teaching and learning take place – the classroom. It also means that we must give attention to the purpose and nature of the tasks and activities that pupils encounter. Our concern is with improving the quality of our teaching in ways that will help all pupils to do well.

The agenda for this book can, therefore, be summarised as a single question. It is:

> How can we help all pupils to
> succeed in the classroom?

In any classroom some pupils will experience difficulties in learning what the teacher is trying to teach. For some pupils this occurs very rarely, for others rather more often, and sadly some seem to experience difficulties much of the time. This is true irrespective of the context. It applies to examination classes in secondary schools as much as it does to a class of 6 and 7 year olds, or even students in higher education.

In addressing the question we will try to remain within the confines of typical classroom conditions. That is, we recognise that most teachers work with thirty pupils or more, and that usually they teach their classes alone. All the ideas and strategies discussed, therefore, can be applied in a general way with a full class; they do not assume that a disproportionate amount of time can, or should, be spent with one or two pupils. We also assume that most teachers are normal people and have better things to do with their time than spend four hours each evening preparing the next day's work.

Finally the book does not set out to provide simple solutions to complicated problems of curriculum and classroom organisation. The uniqueness of each encounter between teacher and pupils is such that prescriptions rarely fit and leave the reader either irritated or, even worse, feeling inadequate. Instead what is provided here is a framework that can be used to review and, we hope, extend and develop our thinking and practice in relation to the central question – how can we help all pupils to succeed in the classroom? We believe that this question is the concern of all teachers and that the framework we provide is equally applicable wherever they work.

Defining success

First of all then we must begin by explaining what we mean when we say 'success'. It is a difficult idea to define precisely not least because it tends to mean different things to different people. In some ways it is easier to state what we don't mean. For example, we don't mean passing examinations. This is, of course, important but, given the narrow focus of the forms of examination used in schools, such a restricted definition consigns vast numbers of youngsters to almost inevitable failure.

For similar reasons we don't mean doing better than the next pupil. Obviously competition for jobs or places in higher education is a fact of life. If, however, learning becomes characterised as solely a matter of competition in which there are winners and losers, some pupils will almost always end up as the losers who therefore have no possibility of success.

And finally, we don't mean never making mistakes. Such a definition would make 'success' both unachievable and, indeed, undesirable.

So, what do we mean by success? There are two strands to our definition. The first of these concerns *self-confidence*. We want pupils to develop a positive and optimistic attitude towards learning and a willingness to tackle unfamiliar challenges in the classroom. As John Holt (1964) said, 'The scared learner is always a poor learner'. The second strand to our definition of success concerns *independence*. By this we mean encouraging pupils to learn more about themselves as learners and to become sensitive to their preferred methods of learning.

In a sense, nurturing self-confidence and independence is a means to an end. The ultimate goal is *to help pupils to take responsibility for their own learning*. Much of the book is influenced by this single idea, which we believe should guide the process of learning from when children first attend school and continue throughout their education.

It is unreasonable and foolish to foist this responsibility upon youngsters at some arbitrarily selected age and expect them to cope.

In summary, therefore, our definition of 'success' is bound up with the pupils' own perceptions of, and subsequent attitudes towards, classroom experiences. Pupils are succeeding if they are becoming more self-confident, better able and more willing to tackle unfamiliar problems independently, and taking an increasing responsibility for their own learning.

Key factors

To recap. We have explained that this book examines ways of helping all pupils to succeed in the classroom. We have defined success in terms of pupils' willingness and ability to take responsibility for their own learning. In the same way that success is attainable for all pupils, all pupils may from time to time experience learning difficulties.

What follows is a framework which is intended to provide readers with a means of reviewing their own thinking and practice. We believe that teachers, like their pupils, should take responsibility for their own learning. The framework provides an indication of those aspects of teaching that we feel should be kept under review. These have been chosen in the belief that it makes sense to pay particular attention to those factors over which we have some significant influence.

The idea of de-emphasising factors and information over which we have little or no influence represents a departure from current thinking for many of us. An example will perhaps illustrate what it means. Some children grow up in a happy, caring and stimulating home; others do not. Some children are taught, by all that is said and done at home, that school is important and teachers are nice, approachable people; others are not. The influence of the home is considerable, and it works both ways.

As teachers we can all think of pupils whose difficulties at school are linked, obviously and directly, to circumstances at home. However, whilst we may be convinced that the cause of learning problems is in the home, the solution – if there is one – is seldom to be found there. Why? Simply because the social and domestic circumstances of the pupils we teach are usually outside our sphere of influence.

In presenting this argument we are certainly not seeking to undermine the importance of effective communication and liaison between school and home. We would also agree that it is helpful for teachers to be aware of important domestic changes and upheavals which may be upsetting pupils in school. We are simply warning against a preoccupation with background domestic information, past or present, which is of neither legitimate concern nor practical relevance to teachers. Concentrating on factors over which we have significant influence rarely, if ever, means concentrating on the domestic affairs of our pupils.

Similarly we need to resist the temptation to seek explanations and solutions to children's difficulties by speculating about the inside of their brains. How often do we hear of pupils having a 'learning blockage', 'mild brain damage', a 'specific learning disability' or 'low intelligence'? Even if it was agreed what any of these phrases mean, which is doubtful, what are we supposed to do about it? Such attempts to explain the causes of children's problems were very much the fashion amongst remedial and special education experts until recently, but are now generally recognised to have been a wild goose chase.

So what are the important factors over which we have an influence? Quite simply, the decisions we take that determine what happens in the classroom. This is not to deny that children's performance in the classroom is affected by other dimensions which may be of a social, emotional, medical or intellectual nature. If, however, these factors are largely beyond our influence they can become a distraction, leading us to underestimate the importance of what happens in school, in our own classrooms.

Our attention, therefore, will be on examining and monitoring the effects of decisions that are made about the curriculum. For the purposes of this discussion we use the term 'curriculum' to refer to all the planned experiences that are provided for the pupils.

Framework for review

The process of reflection which we are keen to encourage teachers to adopt is based on our assumption that the most significant source of learning is personal experience. So, in trying to improve our professional practice as teachers we suggest that all of us need to keep our ways of working under continual review in order to identify areas that are worthy of development. In particular, the aim should be to improve skills in planning and implementing the curriculum in ways that will encourage success for all pupils.

Central to this approach is what we call classroom evaluation, a continuous process of monitoring and reviewing important decisions about what happens in the classroom. An explanation of what this involves is presented in Chapter 2.

Our framework for review provides a map of the three areas to be considered. Together they are a comprehensive agenda for keeping under review those factors over which we have substantial influence. They are summarised in the table on page 9.

The three broad areas – objectives, tasks and activities, and classroom arrangements – are not discrete and independent. Decisions about one cannot be taken without reference to the others. For example, the design of tasks and activities must be linked to pupils' objectives and take account of the arrangement of resources in the classroom. Neither are we suggesting that decisions have to be taken in any particular order. The three areas of decision-making are so inextricably interlinked that often they are made at the same time. They are examined separately here merely for the convenience of writers and reader.

(1) Objectives

The amount of freedom teachers have in making decisions about curriculum objectives varies considerably. Some, whether they like it or not, seem to have virtual autonomy; others have to teach within a curriculum framework that has been adopted as a departmental, school or local authority policy. As we write, this whole area is a matter of considerable debate as a result of government legislation which requires the introduction of a National Curriculum.

Nevertheless, as things stand, we all still have considerable influence over the choice of objectives for our pupils. Even teaching older pupils who are working towards public examinations provides some scope for deciding what is taught and how.

Chapter 3 discusses the issues involved in determining objectives for all pupils. It stresses the importance of clarifying intentions, taking account of the needs of individual pupils, flexibility and keeping objectives under review. Emphasis is placed on pupil involvement as part of a planned policy for helping all pupils to take responsibility for their own learning.

(2) Tasks and activities

For the purposes of discussion we have distinguished between objectives and tasks and activities. 'Tasks and activities' describe what pupils do in the classroom; 'objectives' define the purpose of tasks and activities.

ENCOURAGING CLASSROOM SUCCESS: FRAMEWORK FOR REVIEW

Through the process of *classroom evaluation* (Chapter 2) the following broad areas of decision-making are kept under review:

OBJECTIVES
(Chapter 3)

● How can we determine appropriate objectives for all our pupils?

TASKS AND ACTIVITIES
(Chapter 4)

● How can we help pupils to be actively engaged in the tasks and activities that are set?

CLASSROOM ARRANGEMENTS
(Chapter 5)

● How do we make effective use of the resources available to facilitate learning?

The key issue here is that tasks and activities should be designed in ways that will encourage pupil participation. Important features of teaching that is successful in this respect are the clarification of the nature and purpose of what is planned, the matching of tasks and materials to individual pupils, an emphasis on interest, and the provision of support and feedback.

Chapter 4 examines these issues, emphasising the value of setting tasks and activities in ways that encourage pupils to work cooperatively.

(3) Classroom arrangements

The concern here is with the use of available resources. By resources we are not referring solely, or even mainly, to books and equipment. We are using the term in its broadest sense. For example, pupils can learn from and be supported by one another; pupils are a resource. Some schools enjoy the benefits of encouraging active parental involvement and even using parents as classroom helpers; parents are a resource. Perhaps the most valuable resource, however, is the teacher's own time. All of these resources, if they are to be used to the greatest benefit of all pupils, need to be managed effectively. This is our third area of decision-making.

Chapter 5 looks at these issues with particular reference to the use of time. The need to arrange the classroom in ways that increase the amount of time available for pupils and teachers to interact in ways that facilitate learning is stressed.

Two final points

As we use the framework to consider important areas of decision-making, we will emphasise two points which we believe to be crucial if teaching is to enable pupils to experience feelings of success. These points apply equally to each aspect of our framework – objectives, tasks and activities, and classroom arrangements.

First of all, we must recognise the importance of achieving a reasonable match between the attainments and interests of individual pupils and the activities they are asked to do. Our concern is to take account of their individual differences, particularly with respect to their:

○ **Previous experience**
  Every pupil brings to school a unique range of personal

experience. Looked at from our perspective as teachers the experience of some may seem limited or distorted, perhaps, for example, as a result of the economic circumstances of their families. Nevertheless each pupil has personal knowledge and preferences that can and should be used as a basis for enhancing their learning.

○ **Existing skills and knowledge**
Setting tasks at an appropriate level for each pupil is a fundamental skill of being an effective teacher. Essentially this is a matter of knowing what the child can already do in order to decide what he or she should be asked to do next. This might be at a very obvious level, for example, when a child must be able to count before carrying out tasks involving addition and subtraction of numbers. More often, however, the skills and knowledge necessary for progression to some new educational tasks are complex and difficult to determine.

○ **Attitudes**
On first admission to school most children are eager to learn and explore new experiences. It is sad that this initial enthusiasm and confidence seems to die away in some cases. In considering pupils as individuals we need to be sensitive to their attitudes towards various types of learning tasks. Some may have a negative view of themselves as learners based upon previous experiences of failure; some may also have little confidence in teachers as people who can help them to succeed in learning.

The overall message of all of this, therefore, is that we need to know our pupils as well as possible.

The second point to be kept in mind as we make decisions about the curriculum is the vital importance of understanding. Learning will occur only if those involved have a sense of personal meaning about what is to happen, why and how. Without meaning, classroom tasks and activities simply become routines to be followed because they are required by the teacher. We have to find effective ways of ensuring that our pupils share an understanding of what we have planned in order that they can engage in these activities in a manner that will facilitate their learning.

This leads us to place particular emphasis on the importance of negotiation in the classroom. We believe that where teachers and pupils work collaboratively, sharing in decision-making to a reasonable degree, a greater sense of understanding is likely to be achieved.

In considering decisions about classroom evaluation, objectives, tasks and activities and classroom arrangements, therefore, we stress the point that collaboration is an effective means of facilitating understanding.

In summary, then, the aspects of teaching that feature in the framework for self-review presented in this book were selected because they are areas of decision-making over which we have significant influence. In considering these aspects we will stress the importance of taking account of pupils' individual differences and finding ways of ensuring understanding, since these are critical features of classroom activity which encourage success.

Summary

The growth of remedial and special education provision over the last twenty-five years has been influenced by the assumption that learning difficulties arise largely as a result of the limitations and disabilities of children. Consequently the approaches that have developed have tended to focus attention on individual children, taking little or no account of the contexts within which teaching and learning take place. This orientation has had negative effects on the attitudes and practices of many teachers and has worked to the disadvantage of some of their pupils.

A new orientation is proposed which emphasises the importance of making teaching more effective. The overall aim is to find ways of helping all pupils to experience success in the classroom. Attention is focused on key decisions over which teachers have influence, particularly with respect to the planning and implementation of the curriculum. It is assumed that the most significant source of learning is personal experience. This has implications for the learning of pupils and teachers.

The rest of this book provides a framework that can be used by teachers to review their existing practice. Central to this is the process of classroom evaluation, which involves the monitoring of decisions about objectives, tasks and activities, and classroom arrangements. Throughout, two points are emphasised: first of all the need to take account of each pupil's existing skills, knowledge and interest, and their previous experience; secondly, the importance of ensuring that pupils have an understanding of the purpose and nature of classroom activities.

Recommended further reading

Ainscow, M. (1985). New directions in meeting special needs. *Pastoral Care*, **3**, 1, 38–45.
An overview of recent trends in the special needs field.

Bickel, W. E. and Bickel, D. D. (1986). Effective schools, classrooms and instruction: implications for special education. *Exceptional Children*, **52**, 6, 489–500.
A useful review of recent research evidence. The authors argue that this has important implications for the way in which schools respond to pupils experiencing difficulty.

Bines, H. (1986). *Redefining Remedial Education*. London: Croom Helm.
An examination of new approaches to remedial education from a sociological standpoint.

Gipps, C., Gross, A. and Goldstein, H. (1987). *Warnock's Eighteen Per Cent*. London: Falmer.
The results of research into how local education authorities are developing provision for pupils with special educational needs in the light of recent legislation.

Morsink, C. V., Soar, R. S., Soar, R. M. and Thomas, R. (1986). Research on teaching: Opening the door to special education classrooms. *Exceptional Children*, **53**, 1, 32–40.
Reviews literature on effectiveness in teaching and examines its relevance to pupils with special needs.

Schon, D. (1983). *The Reflective Practitioner*. New York: Basic Books.
A penetrating discussion of the practical implications of professionalism.

Tomlinson, S. (1982). *A Sociology of Special Education*. London. RKP.
Taking a sociological perspective on the development of special education, the author expresses her anxiety that present trends will lead to an increase in the percentage of pupils segregated.

Wang, M. C., Reynolds, M. C. and Walberg, H. J. (1986). Rethinking special education. *Educational Leadership*, **44**, 1, 26–31.
Argues that the emphasis on withdrawing pupils from ordinary classes has led to the neglect of the more important issue of how to improve the quality of regular classroom learning environments.

CHAPTER 2

Classroom Evaluation

We have argued that the most effective means of helping pupils to succeed in the classroom is to concentrate on factors over which we have some influence. In particular, we have identified three critical aspects of planning and implementing the curriculum. These are:

- objectives
- tasks and activities
- classroom arrangements.

It is important to stress that we all make decisions about pupil objectives, tasks and activities, and classroom arrangements constantly – every day, several times a day. Each time we enter the classroom we decide what to teach, the tasks and activities we propose to use, and how we intend organising the classroom. These routine decisions are an integral part of teaching.

These three broad areas of decision-making are interrelated. It is not a question of making decisions in an orderly sequence as though we are programmed to move logically through a flow diagram. Whilst lessons may be planned in some detail in advance, we frequently need to adapt and modify our plans as activities unfold. We therefore make decisions 'on the spot', and often make decisions about all three aspects of our teaching simultaneously.

These decisions should be influenced by two main factors. These are:

(1) Pupils' knowledge, skills, interests and previous experience

This is self-evidently the case when making decisions about objectives. If we set objectives that do not take account of such information, pupils will struggle to make sense of the curriculum. However, decisions about tasks and activities and classroom organisation should also be influenced by pupils' existing knowledge, interests and previous experience.

(2) Pupils' understanding of our decisions

Pupils should understand what they are expected to learn and why. They should understand how to carry out the tasks and activities they are set, and how and why the classroom is organised to allow this to occur. The most effective way of ensuring that pupils understand our decisions is to involve them directly in our decision-making. If this is not always practicable, we should at least make sure that they understand, as far as possible, what we have decided on their behalf.

What does all this mean, for example for the teacher of twenty-nine mixed-ability 10 year olds? We are suggesting that all three aspects of her or his teaching (i.e. objectives, tasks and activities, and classroom arrangements) should be kept under constant review, particularly with regard to pupils' existing skills and knowledge and their understanding of our decisions — for all twenty-nine pupils, all of the time. This is classroom evaluation and the key to encouraging classroom success. It is also extremely difficult!

The remainder of this chapter describes this approach to evaluation in some detail. It is not promoting a radical new way of working involving particular or specialised techniques. *We believe that attitude is infinitely more potent than technique.* In essence, we are promoting an attitude to evaluation which requires an open mind and a commitment to improve our effectiveness as teachers. It is an approach that recognises the complexities of classroom life, and is based on a belief that the most important source of learning, for teachers and pupils, is personal experience.

Classroom evaluation, as we have chosen to define it, has three major attributes. It is . . .

(1) *wide-ranging*
i.e. it is concerned with a much broader perspective than merely monitoring pupils' achievement of objectives.

(2) *a process*
i.e. it is a continuous process that is an integral part of life in the classroom.

(3) *collaborative*
i.e. it necessarily involves colleagues, parents and the pupils themselves.

In the remainder of this chapter, each of these three attributes is discussed in turn and in some detail. It will be seen that this collaborative and wide-ranging process, which we call classroom evaluation, is indistinguishable from a contemporary definition of assessment. In other words, classroom evaluation and assessment are, in fact, one and the same thing. We begin with an explanation of how and why this is so.

A broader view of classroom evaluation

In the field of special and remedial education during the past twenty-five years or so, the meaning of the term 'assessment' has evolved through three quite distinct stages. In the 1960s, assessment was preoccupied with an *analysis of the learner*. There was an assumption that, if the pupil failed to learn, there must be a deficiency in the learner. This led to a plethora of tests that purported to help teachers recognise the relative strengths and weaknesses of the pupil's internal learning processes. It was assumed that these test data enabled us to design individual programmes of activities for pupils which remediated weaknesses and/or built on existing personal strengths. By the early 1970s, however, it had been recognised that this approach – despite its many inherent attractions – was based on unfounded psychological theories and poorly constructed assessment devices. Moreover, the approach encouraged the segregation of some pupils who were thought to be in some way different and in need of specialised educational 'treatment'.

During the 1970s attention switched from an analysis of the learner to *an analysis of the task*. Now the emphasis was placed on analysing tasks within the curriculum into incremental steps, with a view to matching objectives to the existing skills of the individual pupil. An advantage of this approach, with which we have been strongly associated in the past, was that it encouraged us to take a more optimistic outlook. Instead of focusing on pupils' difficulties and limitations, we were seeking to overcome these by careful curriculum planning. However, a disadvantage of the approach was that it still tended to lead to some pupils working on separate activities and being denied curriculum opportunities that were offered to others.

The approach we are recommending in this book does not abandon the need to match the curriculum to the existing skills and knowledge of the learner. We are suggesting, however, that merely to analyse what is being taught and match this to the attainments of the learner is too narrow a perspective. We are proposing, instead, an *analysis of the learning environment*. In particular, we are suggesting that such an analysis should focus on objectives, tasks and activities, and classroom arrangements; and that these should be reviewed in terms of pupils' knowledge, skills, interests and previous experience, and their understanding of our decisions.

To summarise, the meaning of 'assessment' in the field of special and remedial education has evolved through three quite distinct stages. In the 1960s we were preoccupied with analysing the individual child; in the 1970s the emphasis was switched to analysing tasks within the curriculum; and now we believe we should be focusing on the learning environment. Such an analysis is synonymous with what we are calling 'classroom evaluation'.

This evolution of the meaning of the term 'assessment' has run parallel to, and is compatible with, developments in evaluation in education generally. Not so many years ago, the evaluation literature was dominated by what has been called the 'classical model' of evaluation (e.g. Tyler, 1949; Wheeler, 1967). This approach required broad curriculum aims to be converted into specific objectives which were described as observable actions (i.e. behavioural or performance objectives). This provided a basis for evaluation. In other words, we knew what the pupil was intended to be able to do following instruction, and could therefore measure how successful our teaching had been in terms of bringing about these learning outcomes. Some even argued (e.g. Popham, 1975) that evaluation without clear objectives was impossible.

This traditional or 'classical' approach to evaluation, of course, is entirely compatible with the use of objectives in curriculum planning. It implies that the curriculum itself should be used as a means of evaluating the effectiveness of teaching. However, in recent years, the shortcomings of the approach have become increasingly apparent.

To focus solely on curriculum objectives and the extent to which they have been achieved by pupils is to risk ignoring different but equally important information. We have discussed already in this chapter a wide range of issues which we believe should be kept under constant review. These extend well beyond merely monitoring pupils' progress towards the achievement of objectives.

There is also the question of unintended outcomes. When we set out to teach a group of pupils with a clear purpose, the unexpected often happens. We may have modest success in teaching what we set out to teach, but in the process reap benefits that were neither planned nor anticipated. Conversely, an activity may be successful in helping pupils achieve their objectives but carry with it unplanned and undesirable outcomes. If the teaching process is evaluated purely in terms of our success in helping pupils to achieve particular objectives, we may not take into account unplanned and unanticipated outcomes – both desirable and undesirable. Clearly, evaluation must be broader in its focus than this traditional approach.

In recognition of these limitations and difficulties associated with the classical approach to evaluation, recent years have seen a definite move towards more flexible and wide-ranging approaches. The aim has been to seek ways of evaluating educational activities so that the complex nature of the classroom is more effectively reflected. We believe that a broader perspective is provided by appraising (a) the objectives set for pupils, (b) the tasks and activities in which they are engaged, and (c) the classroom arrangements made to facilitate the learning of the pupils. These factors need to be reviewed in the light of pupils' existing skills and knowledge, and their understanding of the nature and purpose of the activities with which they are engaged.

Classroom evaluation as a process

It should be clear by now that we do not see evaluation as a 'one-off' event in which classroom life stops in order that evaluation can 'be done'. Neither is classroom evaluation the day in the school calendar on which the Head Teacher administers a reading test to the whole school.

Instead we believe that classroom evaluation is the responsibility of all teachers and should be an integral and crucial aspect of teaching. Evaluation is a continuous process which involves reflecting upon and interpreting events and activities in the classroom, as they happen. More than anything else, therefore, evaluation requires an attitude of mind that seeks out relevant information and responds to events as they occur.

All of this sounds rather grand and perhaps, for some readers, somewhat intimidating. We would stress, however, that we are not suggesting that any radically different approach be adopted. We are arguing simply that we look for ways of improving our capacity to learn from, and respond to, our own classroom experiences.

It is helpful to break down the process of evaluation into three constituent components. These are not discrete or independent elements and, in practice, overlap and even occur simultaneously.

They are:

(1) information gathering
(2) review
(3) action.

Let us consider these three aspects of the evaluation process in more detail.

(1) Information gathering

What kind of information should we be gathering? In broad terms, there are two kinds: the intended and the unintended. In other words, did what was planned occur and did anything else of importance happen?

Returning to the three aspects of curriculum planning referred to earlier, an evaluation of planned or intended outcomes gives rise to three broad questions:

● Are objectives being achieved?
● Are tasks and activities being completed?
● Do classroom arrangements make effective use of available resources?

More specifically, we should be questioning whether the decisions we make under these three broad headings take adequate account of pupils' existing skills, knowledge and interests, and the extent to which these decisions are understood by our pupils.

And finally, remembering our concern with unintended outcomes, we should add a fourth question:

● What else is happening?

Throughout this book we argue consistently for the greater involvement of pupils in planning, evaluating performance and record keeping. There is surely no better way of ensuring pupils' understanding of our decisions than involving them directly in our decision-making. Collecting information about these four questions, therefore, should involve us in talking to pupils, and pupils talking to each other, about the activities in which they are engaged. This point is taken up in some detail in the next section.

To be involved in effective classroom evaluation, we need to keep these four questions in mind as we teach. However, such information is only worth collecting if it is used.

(2) Review

Evaluative information concerning classroom events and activities should be analysed and reviewed by all those involved. This process must be collaborative; it must involve teacher *and* pupils. In other words, we should ask pupils for their opinions about their work, rather than relying on our interpretations of their reactions. Sharing perceptions in this way is vital because they are frequently different.

What are the important features of classrooms where this idea of reflection is emphasised? Most obviously, there is a lot of discussion between pupils and teacher, and between pupils and pupils, about the work being undertaken in class. Central to the ethos created in the classroom is the powerful message that the point of view of every individual is valued.

This approach to reviewing classroom activities depends more on an appropriate attitude than high-powered technique. In other words, pupils should be encouraged to formulate and articulate their own views, even though they may not always be positive. This requires openness, and an acceptance of criticism, on our part. Providing an opportunity to express their views is often sufficient for some pupils; others may need considerable support and encouragement. Questions should be open-ended, assumptions should be challenged, and pupils should be encouraged to justify their opinions.

Creating such an ethos may take time, particularly with pupils who are not accustomed to their views being sought and apparently valued. In this situation, a useful procedure is to set time aside for the formulation of questions. So, for example, the teacher may spend some time introducing a topic, and then ask pupils to work in pairs or small groups with the specific task of identifying issues for further discussion and attention.

In general, strategies that require pupils to consider the significance of what they are doing are an essential feature of effective classroom evaluation. This can take many forms. In one primary school we know children are encouraged to talk to one another at various points during the day about what they have been doing, what they have achieved and how they feel. By the time they get to the age of 11 many of them have developed a sophisticated view of themselves as learners and are well able to describe their own strengths and weaknesses, preferences and interests in considerable detail.

The process of reflecting on learning may also be carried out in written form. For example, some teachers of English like to write comments and messages to pupils in reply to their creative writing. These are intended to create a dialogue rather than the more traditional approach of making qualitative judgements. Thus they may lead to an interchange of ideas between teacher and pupil in which they share quite private and personal thoughts with one another. For teenagers, in particular, this may encourage a form of expression with which they might otherwise feel uncomfortable. Once again, this approach reinforces the point that the teacher values the pupil's opinion.

Another strategy which we have seen used very effectively with pupils of different ages involves keeping a 'learning journal'. This is a diary, a personal document which the pupil may or may not wish to share with friends or the teacher. Essentially, the idea is to encourage pupils to take more responsibility for their own learning. Time is allocated during the day for making entries, which must relate to aspects of classroom work. One teacher, known to the authors, provided the following subheadings as guidelines for pupils:

Ideas that you would like to remember
Questions that you need to think about
Leads to follow up
Points to share with your friends
Reactions to your lessons

In addition to pupils reflecting on their activities and experiences we are also keen to encourage teachers to take a reflective view of their own work. This may well be facilitated by interchange with pupils in some of the ways we have described. It is also important, however, that time is found to talk with colleagues about matters of common concern. Where this works well it can be one of the most enriching aspects of various types of collaborative teaching. Planning classroom activities together, sharing in their implementation, and reviewing the outcomes can be a tremendous source of professional development. Indeed, our experience has been that a feature of successful schools is an emphasis on discussion of teaching and learning.

(3) Action

Gathering and reviewing information are pointless if they do not lead to some form of action. This is where the need for flexibility is so vital, and the demands on the teacher can be so great.

We are assuming that, having set out with a plan of action for a lesson or series of lessons, we are prepared to review and modify this in the light of how it goes in the classroom. So, decisions that were made beforehand can be changed or modified as a consequence of what happens in the classroom and how people feel as activities develop. Objectives may be changed, tasks and activities modified, and classrooms reorganised as part of a continuous process of classroom evaluation.

Collaboration and classroom evaluation

We have emphasised the wide-ranging nature of evaluation and stressed that it is an integral part of teaching. We would also argue that, for classroom evaluation to be effective, it should involve teachers working collaboratively with one another, with parents and with the pupils themselves.

This suggestion demands a considerable change of outlook by many of those involved. Traditionally, schooling has been seen as an enterprise in which those who know, the teachers, attempt to pass on what they know to those who don't, the pupils. The responsibility for planning, implementing and evaluating this process was the teachers'. The pupils' role was passive as recipients of the information; parents were kept at arm's length and told what teachers thought they should know; and even our own colleagues didn't get to know much about what we did in our own classroom. Our proposals for classroom evaluation are as far away from this bleak portrait of yesteryear as it is possible to get.

Our definition of classroom success underlined the importance of pupils increasing their willingness and ability to take responsibility for their own learning. The aim is to help pupils to become more self-confident and independent in all learning situations. In order for this to happen they must have access to information and, indeed, be encouraged to comment upon and interpret this information from their own perspectives.

There are other important arguments, however, for involving pupils in the evaluation process. For example, engaging pupils in discussions and negotiations is an effective strategy for helping them to understand the nature and purpose of their work. Understanding has a positive effect on motivation. All of us are more likely to invest effort and commitment into enterprises that have meaning and significance. Regrettably it is not all that uncommon to watch pupils engage in classroom tasks without any apparent understanding of the purpose of the exercise – except that they understand that it is the teacher's will that they do it!

Collaborating with pupils in the evaluation process can also have benefits in terms of classroom organisation and the management of time. Collaboration means sharing responsibility. This should lead to pupils being less dependent on teachers for making routine administrative and organisational decisions on their behalf – decisions that pupils should be encouraged to take for themselves. A reduction in pupils' dependency should, in turn, ease the demands on the teacher, leaving time to focus on other, more important aspects of classroom organisation.

Whenever possible, collaboration in the evaluation process should involve working and cooperating with colleagues. Again, it is a question of sharing responsibility, of casting the net wide in a search for views and perspectives regarding the outcomes of classroom activities. We would argue that the process is more enjoyable and certainly enriched if it is undertaken jointly by two or more teachers, perhaps team teaching or teaching the same course to different groups of pupils.

What we said earlier about access of information regarding pupils applies just as much to parents. We should be seeking ways of involving parents actively, providing information about what we are trying to teach and how we are going about it. Such a dialogue should include an evaluation of the progress being made and problems being encountered.

There is one final, important benefit of collaboration. Teaching can be an extremely stressful profession. It is made more stressful if important decisions about the development and delivery of the curriculum are taken in isolation. Working collaboratively with colleagues and pupils is not only likely to improve the quality of our decisions as teachers, it can also decrease the pressures and stresses that working in isolation can generate.

Finding ways of working closely with colleagues and, wherever possible, parents is therefore a sensible way of building a personal support network. Throughout this book we emphasise the importance of seeing other adults as a source of support. This can only be achieved by being prepared to share information, respect the knowledge and views of others and negotiate in a reasonably flexible manner.

Summary

Success in the classroom is more likely to occur if objectives, tasks and activities, and classroom arrangements take account of individual pupils and are understood by all those involved.

Classroom evaluation is a process of monitoring and reviewing these aspects as the curriculum is planned and enacted. It also involves taking note of significant unintended outcomes. This approach has three interrelated elements: 'information gathering', which is concerned with noting what happens in the classroom; 'review', which is to do with analysing and interpreting this information; and 'action', which involves responding accordingly.

It is important that classroom evaluation is seen as a continuous process, built into the normal life of the classroom. Collaboration between teachers, pupils and, where possible, parents is also vital. The approach is based on the assumption that the most important source of learning for teachers and pupils is their own experiences.

In the next three chapters we look in turn at what we have defined as the three crucial aspects of decision-making: objectives, tasks and activities and classroom arrangements. As we do so it is important to remember that these are interrelated. It is also necessary to keep in mind the point that, whilst such decisions are often made before a lesson or activity commences, they can be modified or, indeed, abandoned as things proceed.

Recommended further reading

Elliott, J. (1981). *Action Research: Framework for Self-evaluation in Schools.* Cambridge Institute of Education, mimeo.
A useful introductory paper on action research. Provides a useful basis for teachers wishing to investigate aspects of their own practice.

Good, T. L. and Brophy, J. E. (1984). *Looking in Classrooms.* New York: Harper & Row.
An excellent source book on techniques of classroom observation and suggestions for influencing the interests, learning and social development of pupils positively.

Hopkins, D. (1985). *A Teacher's Guide to Classroom Research.* Milton Keynes: Open University.
A clear, concise book in which the author provides practical advice on how teachers can improve their own teaching by engaging in classroom research.

Iano, R. P. (1986). The study and development of teaching: With implications for the advancement of special education. *Remedial and Special Education,* **7,** 5, 50-61.
The author of this article is critical of much of the research on teaching that has been carried out. He argues for an alternative orientation which would promote a genuine tradition of inquiry amongst teachers.

McCormick, R. and James, M. (1988). *Curriculum Evaluation in Schools.* London: Croom Helm.
In addition to providing a detailed account of recent developments in the field of educational evaluation, this book offers some practical help in developing strategies for improving teaching and learning.

Stenhouse, L. (1975). *An Introduction to Curriculum Research and Development.* London: Heinemann.
An excellent account of key issues in the curriculum, particularly with respect to evaluation. Stresses the idea of teachers as researchers.

Taylor, P. H. and Richards, C. M. (1985). *An Introduction to Curriculum Studies.* Windsor: NFER-Nelson.
A useful introductory textbook which provides a basis for further study of curriculum theory.

Walker, R. (1985). *Doing Research: A Handbook for Teachers.* London: Methuen.
Another useful source book on methods that can be used to evaluate teaching and learning.

Ysseldyke, J. E. and Christenson, S. L. (1987). Evaluating students' instructional environments. *Remedial and Special Education,* **8,** 3, 17-24.
Proposes an approach to assessment that is largely consistent with that described in this chapter.

CHAPTER 3

Objectives

If you have the privilege of observing a number of competent and confident teachers at work with their classes you are likely to recognise a number of common features in what they do. Possibly the most significant of these is the noticeable sense of purpose that characterises their activities. As they set up tasks and activities and interact with their pupils they seem to have a clear idea of what they want their classes to achieve. Furthermore these intentions appear to be understood and shared by the members of the class.

When discussing our teaching intentions or the purpose of classroom activities, we are in effect talking about objectives. In this chapter, therefore, we look at the question:

> How can we determine appropriate
> objectives for all our pupils?

This discussion revisits the debate about the use of objectives as a means of curriculum planning.

For many years, textbooks about curriculum design have included sections about objectives. Some have argued that setting out the curriculum in terms of specific objectives is essential to effective learning; others have suggested that such forms of planning are contrary to the principles of good education. It is important to recognise that rarely, if ever, is it suggested that there should not be purpose and intention in the classroom, but simply that stating objectives in a very detailed way can have a limiting effect on the way in which the curriculum is enacted.

Our contribution to this debate so far has not been with respect to curriculum development in a general sense. In a range of earlier publications (e.g. Ainscow and Tweddle, 1979 and 1984), we have presented strategies for using objectives as a means of providing intensive help to individual pupils who are experiencing difficulties in learning. We have come to recognise, however, that whilst these approaches can be highly effective in certain situations they have severe limitations and, indeed, possible dangers. One of these problems is that a preoccupation with the analysis of curriculum content into sequences of objectives can – if we are not very careful – distract us from other equally important issues, such as tasks and activities and classroom arrangements.

In considering how objectives should be planned, therefore, we will be examining these difficulties and making some recommendations as to how they might be avoided.

Objectives and learning difficulties

Our own work in developing what has come to be regarded as the 'objectives approach' to children's learning difficulties grew out of the experience of developing the curriculum in a special school during the 1970s. Some of the principles and strategies were then used as a means of helping individual pupils in primary and secondary schools.

Put simply, the approach requires the development of teaching programmes based on priorities within the curriculum for a pupil or group of pupils experiencing difficulties in learning. Considerable attention is given to assessing the existing capabilities of the pupils in order to set learning priorities that can be achieved in a relatively short period of time. Priorities are defined in terms of learning objectives stated as observable behaviours that are to be the intended outcomes of the activities presented to the pupils. Such objectives, sometimes known as behavioural or performance objectives, are seen as targets to be achieved and criteria against which progress can be measured.

We know of many examples where teachers use this form of planning with considerable success as a means of helping children to make progress where previously they had been struggling. A common feature of these examples is that the process of planning with objectives has the effect of raising expectations of what might be achieved.

In practical terms, the main advantages of planning objectives-based programmes for pupils experiencing learning difficulties might be summarised as follows:

THEY
- help us to match tasks and activities to the existing attainments of individual pupils;
- provide a focus for giving additional attention and support;
- lead us to have a more positive expectation of what can be achieved;
- provide a basis for monitoring progress on a continuous basis.

We would also wish to add that when we have seen the approach used most effectively it has been in contexts where there has been a strong emphasis on collaborative planning. Indeed, we tend to take the view that this process of working together may be the key feature and it is one that is emphasised throughout this book.

Limitations of the objectives approach

In reflecting on our experience over many years using objectives to plan the curriculum for pupils experiencing difficulties in learning, we have become sensitive to some of the limitations of this approach. We would like to discuss these issues before providing some positive recommendations regarding how objectives can be used as part of a broader and more flexible approach to planning.

We will examine what seem to us to be the five main difficulties associated with the objectives approach as it has become popular in the field of special needs. These problems are not exclusive to the use of objectives but they can be exacerbated by this approach. In general these can be summarised as follows:

USING OBJECTIVES CAN LEAD TO:
- narrowing of the curriculum
- segregation of pupils
- teachers feeling inadequate
- pupils being passive
- the curriculum becoming static.

Let us look at these five difficulties in a little more detail.

(1) Narrowing of the curriculum

Traditionally the approaches used in many schools for dealing with those pupils perceived as having learning difficulties have reduced the range of educational experiences with which they were presented. The assumption was that it was in their best interests for them not to have to face challenges that were beyond their capabilities. Often this led to an emphasis on the so-called basic skills of reading, writing and arithmetic, providing a curriculum that was, as Brennan (1974) argued, arid, repetitive and lacking in excitement.

We can recall examples of where teachers using an objectives approach have fallen back into this pattern of devising programmes and activities which, though logical in design, lack meaning, purpose and interest for the pupils.

(2) Segregation of pupils

Often associated with this narrowing of the curriculum is the tendency to make some form of separate arrangements for those pupils experiencing difficulties in learning. This may take the form of special classes or withdrawal groups in which members lose the stimulus of working with more successful pupils. It can also mean a more subtle form of separation within the classroom when certain children are working on individual tasks that emphasise their differences from the majority of their classmates.

Setting separate objectives, particularly when this leads pupils to work on different tasks or materials, can further emphasise the segregated status of some pupils.

(3) Teachers feeling inadequate

Earlier we referred to the raised expectations that often seem to characterise situations in which teachers have worked out specific objectives to guide their work with individual pupils experiencing learning difficulties. Sometimes it can lead to a very different reaction. When the notion of planning with objectives has been presented as a set of strict rules to be followed – a sort of 'science of instruction' – teachers can feel intimidated. Associated with this may be feelings of inadequacy about their own competence to deal with certain of their pupils.

(4) Pupils being passive

An emphasis on careful planning of programmes of objectives can encourage us to perceive pupils as having little or no role to play in making decisions about their own learning. Once again this is an attitude of mind that has tended to characterise traditional practice in many schools. It is part of the attempt to provide certain pupils with positive discrimination by protecting them. Unfortunately, even quite young children may sense this attitude and adopt roles that confirm the teacher's expectations. It is an example of what is sometimes called a 'self-fulfilling prophecy'. An associated outcome may be the creation of a sense of dependency within which the pupil only carries out tasks when asked to do so and in the way that is demanded.

(5) The curriculum becoming static

Given that change is often a difficult process in such a complex environment as a school or classroom, there is an obvious danger that, having spent so much time in planning an individual programme, it is difficult to make modifications. It may be, however, that the plan proves to be inadequate or becomes redundant as a result of unexpected circumstances arising. Consequently, pupils may be required to fit into the programme rather than the programme being set as a response to individual needs.

Whilst recognising these difficulties, we would wish to reiterate the point that many teachers have found planning with objectives to be a valuable strategy for helping individual pupils.

Determining objectives

The main thrust of our argument in this chapter is concerned with objectives in a much wider sense, as part of an approach to teaching and learning that attempts to encourage success for all pupils in the classroom. In taking this perspective we are moving away from strategies that are intended to help individual pupils overcome *their* difficulties to an approach that seeks to prevent difficulties from occurring as a result of the decisions we make in our work as teachers. Agreeing objectives is one of a series of interrelated decisions that are made before and during the encounters that occur in the classroom. These decisions have a crucial effect on pupils' learning. Indeed we are committed to the view that an understanding of purpose is an essential element of successful teaching and learning. There have to be objectives or we are, as Barrow (1984) suggests, 'sailing rudderless'.

We are aware, therefore, of the dangers of setting up rigid structures which have the potential for narrowing the focus of education and closing our minds to incidents and opportunities that might stimulate learning. This being the case we would make the following recommendations as to how objectives should be determined:

(1) use objectives as a means of clarifying intentions;
(2) take account of individual pupils;
(3) be flexible; and
(4) keep objectives under review.

Let us look at these four recommendations in more detail.

(1) Clarifying intentions

As we have already argued, effective teaching is characterised by a sense of purpose. It involves teachers working with objectives in mind that help them plan classroom encounters, direct activities and monitor progress. The nature of the objectives will, of course, vary – what they are about, how they are stated and when. The important factor is that a sense of purpose exists.

A sense of purpose may simply mean introducing a lesson or activity by outlining what is going to happen and what it is intended the pupils will achieve. A strategically timed restatement of that purpose can re-focus the attention of pupils and sharpen their understanding. At the end of the session, the activity and the pupils' work can be reviewed by reference back to a further restatement of the purpose.

The process of determining objectives can be a more complex and, at times, subtle affair. Sometimes purposes may be negotiated with a class or individual pupils within a general theme or area of study that is being taught. It may even be the case that the outcomes of an activity may not be clarified until it is completed. Here a process of review would be necessary in order to consider questions such as, what has been important in what we have been doing? or what have we learnt today that has been significant?

Whatever the orientation to determining objectives, it is important that intentions are communicated to the pupils. Our view of objectives is that they are a language to aid the planning and communication of educational purposes. What is essential is that everybody involved – teachers and pupils – understands what is intended and shares some commitment to its achievement. So often when things go badly in classrooms it seems to grow out of a lack of shared understanding about purpose.

(2) Individual pupils

In determining objectives for a class or group the difficult task is to take account of the needs of individual pupils. To restate what we said in Chapter 2, this means recognising and responding to pupils' previous experiences, their existing skills and knowledge, their interests and their attitudes.

Clearly it is essential that we know our pupils as well as possible. Getting to know them takes time and is a demanding process, particularly in secondary schools where teachers might meet four or even more different classes in one day. Consequently the process may need to be accelerated by setting particular tasks as a means of collecting information about pupils quickly as a basis for planning.

This issue points to a further benefit of the process of teacher/pupil collaboration which we are seeking to encourage. If we can find ways of involving pupils in decision-making about their own objectives, their knowledge of themselves can be utilised as a means of responding to their individuality. All of this, of course, demands a relationship between teacher and taught that enables such negotiations to take place – an issue to which we will need to return.

(3) Flexibility

Given that we see objectives as a language for planning and communicating intentions, it is important that the users of the language remain firmly in control of the way in which it is used. The nature of any language is that it is dynamic, changing to suit the needs of those who use it.

During courses and workshops, therefore, we encourage groups of teachers to plan their objectives in ways that suit their own approaches to teaching, taking into account the needs of their pupils. The literature abounds with guidelines for writing objectives (including our own earlier publications), but these should be disregarded if they prove to be inappropriate. The way in which objectives should be stated, the degree of specificity that is necessary and how objectives relate to one another are all matters of teacher judgement. There are no rules; objectives are good objectives if they help you and your pupils to succeed.

In order to maintain breadth in the curriculum it is helpful to bear in mind the range of outcomes, activities and tasks with which we are concerned. In addition to the skills, knowledge and understanding that we want our pupils to acquire, we must be concerned with the development of their personal attitudes, values and interests. It is also important to provide an appropriate range of diverse and stimulating learning contexts in which they can participate. A variety of forms of objectives will be necessary to communicate these broad areas of development. Sometimes, objectives may consist of a fairly specific statement of an intended learning outcome; for example, 'As a result of this series of lessons I expect you to be able to explain the changes in approaches to painting that occurred during the sixteenth century', or 'By Friday I will expect you to be able to spell the words on this list.' Other times it is more appropriate to make rather general statements of intent; for example, 'This activity is intended to help you to get better at making decisions in groups.' Elsewhere a description of the activity that is to take place may well suffice; for example, 'We are going to write stories about what happened when we went on the school trip to the seaside.' Here discussion about what has been achieved would occur during and after the task has been completed.

In summary, we are suggesting that we should plan objectives flexibly, determining them in ways which help everyone involved to understand the purpose of what is to take place.

(4) Review

We have stressed the importance of keeping important decisions about the curriculum under continuous review. This is what classroom evaluation is all about. Indeed, the focus of this chapter has been the question:

> How can we determine appropriate
> objectives for all our pupils?

In particular, we should be asking whether pupils understand their own objectives and are therefore clear about the purposes of the activities in which they are engaged. And we should be seeking to ensure that objectives take account of pupils' existing skills, knowledge, interests and previous experience. Essential to this process is engaging pupils in discussions about their perceptions and interpretations of the purpose of tasks and activities.

Recent years have seen a considerable debate in education about how progress should be assessed and recorded, particularly in secondary schools (e.g. Broadfoot, 1986). This has led to some interesting developments which have major implications for the ways in which we review progress towards the achievement of objectives.

The debate is a product of the fairly widespread dissatisfaction with existing practice. It has been argued, for example, that traditional approaches to record-keeping in schools have failed to motivate a substantial proportion of pupils. A further criticism, which may be linked to this point, is that traditional systems have not involved pupils, directly and actively, in the process. Recent developments in this field have, therefore, sought to increase pupils' levels of motivation by encouraging their active participation in reviewing their own progress.

It has also been argued that the range of achievement recorded in schools has tended to focus on a relatively narrow range of learning outcomes. So, for example, in primary schools assessment of progress can be solely concerned with recording children's achievements in mechanical aspects of reading, spelling and arithmetic. Given that what is recorded has a strong influence on the style and content of what is taught, there is an obvious danger that a narrow focus may lead to limiting of the curriculum opportunities that are provided. Whatever a school's commitment to such rhetoric as 'providing a broad and balanced curriculum', the message that comes through to teachers, pupils and parents is that what is really important is what is assessed!

The dangers of emphasising too narrow a range of outcomes as being important tend to be exacerbated when the form and content of what is to be recorded are pre-determined. So, for example, in some of the early attempts to introduce profile records into secondary schools some years ago, pupil progress was recorded against a set of desired achievements (e.g. 'Can use simple punctuation correctly'). Although these approaches were a considerable step forward in the practice of many schools, they carried with them a narrowness of perspective that could be very limiting if used inflexibly.

There is a clear trend in many of the recent initiatives regarding assessment and recording to relate new approaches more closely to the curriculum in order that information collected can influence what happens in the classroom on a continuous basis. New examinations schemes such as the Oxford Certificate of Educational Achievement (OCEA) are based on this principle (Willmott, 1986). Throughout there is a strong emphasis on pupil self-recording and negotiated assessment involving pupils and teachers. Discussion is facilitated by various recording schedules which they are required to complete collaboratively.

Clearly this type of approach to reviewing and recording learning makes considerable demands on all those involved and necessitates a high degree of flexibility in classroom organisation and openness in discussion. It is perhaps also worth adding that the actual schedules completed may be of less importance than the processes they facilitate. Self-assessment, discussion and negotiated learning objectives are aspects of these processes which can have a positive effect on pupils' attitudes to their work in school.

In discussing these developments we set out not to prescribe a system of record-keeping, but rather to provide some useful leads that might be adapted and incorporated into your existing practice.

In summary, then, we are recommending that forms of reviewing and recording should be developed that:

- ○ can be used continuously;
- ○ are closely related to the curriculum;
- ○ recognise a wide range of achievement;
- ○ are concerned with the process and outcomes of learning; and
- ○ encourage pupil involvement.

These recommendations represent a considerable change of outlook about recording and assessment in schools generally. With respect to the way in which teachers assess the progress of pupils experiencing difficulties in learning they represent a revolution.

Summary

Essential to effective teaching and learning is a sense of purpose which is shared by teachers and pupils. This is to do with determining objectives.

In the field of special needs, objectives have tended to be used as a means of devising individual programmes within the curriculum for pupils perceived as experiencing learning difficulties. This approach has had the effect of raising many teachers' expectations of what can be achieved. It can, however, lead to certain difficulties.

What is recommended, therefore, is an approach to objectives that involves clarifying intentions; taking account of individual pupils; flexibility; and keeping objectives under review.

Recommended further reading

Barrow, R. (1984). *Giving Teaching Back to Teachers*. Brighton: Wheatsheaf.
In this superbly argued book the author concludes that much of the research that has been carried out on teaching and learning is methodologically suspect. His own orientation is summed up by his title. Well worth reading.

Broadfoot, P. (ed.) (1986). *Profiles and Records of Achievements*. London: Holt, Rinehart & Winston.
This collection of papers provides a useful introduction to recent trends in developing new approaches to recording progress in schools.

Gersch, I. (1987). Involving pupils in their own assessment, in T. Bowers (ed.), *Special Educational Needs and Human Resource Management*. London: Croom Helm.
Argues the case for greater pupil involvement in assessment and, indeed, school life in general.

Hull, R. (1985). *The Language Gap*. London: Methuen.
Basing his argument on observations carried out in secondary classrooms, the author indicates the crucial relationship between language and learning. He suggests that teacher talk often seems to get in the way of learning.

Pratt, D. (1980). *Curriculum: Design and Development*. New York: Harcourt Brace Jovanovich.
A textbook for those involved in curriculum design. Recommends a flexible use of objectives.

Wells, G. (1986). *The Meaning Makers: Children Using Language and Using Language to Learn*. London: Hodder & Stoughton.
Based on the evidence of extensive research, the author makes some important suggestions as to how teachers can help their pupils to find meaning and purpose in classroom activities.

CHAPTER 4

Tasks and Activities

It is hardly surprising to find that research indicates that those pupils who make least progress in schools are those who spend least time engaged in the tasks and activities set by their teachers. Teachers have known that since schools were invented. The question is: what do we do about it?

The issue is, of course, a little more complex than that. For example, do some pupils make less progress because they do less work, or do they do less because they feel that they have no real chance of success? Common sense suggests that in many instances the two factors are interrelated.

In this chapter we will be addressing the question:

> How can we help pupils to be actively
> engaged in the tasks and activities that
> are set?

Clearly this involves a range of factors. In the main, however, we will be concentrating on a limited number of these, selected on the basis of our experience and an analysis of the way in which successful teachers operate.

Individual needs

Finding ways of setting tasks and activities that are appropriate for all members of a group or class is part of the wider issue of responding to pupils as individuals. Once again it reminds us of the need to recognise that each pupil enters the classroom with a unique range of personal experiences, attainments, attitudes and interests. It is impossible to take all of these into account but some teachers do seem to have ways of accommodating the diversity of needs represented in their classes to a reasonable degree. What, then, are the key elements of what they do?

In broad terms, the two features of the work of effective teachers which are most critical are those which are stressed throughout this book. They are to do with finding ways of ensuring pupils' understanding of the nature and purpose of the activities in which they are engaged, and checking that these are reasonably matched to their existing attainments and interests.

In the rest of this chapter we will be keeping these two critical aspects of teaching in mind as we consider in more detail the ways in which tasks are set in the classroom. Our argument is that pupils are much more likely to be actively engaged in their work if they understand what they are doing and if they find their tasks challenging, interesting and realistic.

It is, perhaps, useful at this stage to distinguish between objectives and activities. Objectives are concerned with the underlying purpose of an activity, and in Chapter 3 are described as a means of communicating and agreeing that purpose with pupils. In other words, pupils need to be able to answer the question:

Why am I doing this?

Ensuring that pupils understand our decisions about tasks and activities should involve them being able to answer a different question, namely:

Why am I doing it in this way?

The distinction is an important one and should be extended to take account of pupils' attainments and interests.

Chapter 3 argues that our decisions about objectives should be based on a detailed acquaintance with our pupils, their existing knowledge, previous experience and so on. The choice of tasks and activities should be similarly influenced. It is possible to have an appropriate objective – but to use an entirely inappropriate classroom activity. For example, group working assumes that children know *how* to work effectively as a group. There is no doubt that, in this respect, some pupils need very much more guidance and support than others.

All of this adds to the burden of the teacher. We are arguing that pupils should understand not only what they are trying to achieve, but also why they are going about it the way in which they are. We are suggesting, also, that pupils' individuality should be taken into account not only when setting objectives, but also in the choice of appropriate tasks and classroom activities. This means setting aside time to talk to pupils, providing explanations, giving support and feedback, and – perhaps most important of all – *encouraging pupils to formulate and articulate their own views.* In our interactions with pupils it is unfortunate that we tend to be rather better at talking than listening.

In addition to checking pupils' understanding of their tasks we also need to find ways of ensuring that tasks set relate to their existing levels of achievement and interests. Our aim must be to present them with challenges that capture their interest, stimulate their enthusiasm and guide their energies in appropriate directions. Often when pupils are unenthusiastic about their classroom tasks they will refer to them as being boring or irrelevant. 'What's the point?' they will ask. Like it or not, part of our work as teachers is to entertain. This is not to argue that education should be judged on its showbusiness appeal but simply to make the point that each of us is more likely to feel motivated if the task in hand has some personal appeal. There is no evidence as far as we are aware to suggest that learning has to be painful.

The business of setting tasks that are matched to the existing attainments of pupils is an aspect of teaching that most of us find a problem. In large classes particularly, it represents a continual source of pressure and it is almost inevitable that we will not always get it right. This means that sometimes pupils *do* spend time working on activities that are well within their competence and that tend to leave them feeling rather bored or unstimulated. As well, there are times when particular activities or materials prove to be beyond the reach of certain pupils. Clearly, the aim must be to pitch tasks at levels that make demands that each pupil in a class can achieve, provided he or she makes the effort. Accepting that this is not always possible, we must ensure that our classrooms are organised in ways that take this into account. So, for example, when pupils are faltering with activities about which they are uncertain or confused we need to have ways of providing support and feedback.

Competitive and individualised learning

In presenting our thoughts on task setting we must acknowledge the work of David and Roger Johnson (1986) and Robert Slavin (1983), whose ideas have had a considerable effect upon our view of classroom life. In particular, their ideas about the ways in which pupils can help one another to learn, in our view, have considerable implications for encouraging success in the classroom.

Traditionally, much of schooling has been seen as a competition designed to see which pupils can learn the most. It is as though learning is like climbing a ladder to success, the top of which can be achieved only by a privileged few. This idea has been encouraged by writers in certain elements of the popular press who appear to be convinced that competition in schools is a proven strategy for improving educational standards.

Some teachers encourage this view by the ways in which they grade performance and record progress. They set up activities which require their pupils to compete with one another in order to see who is best. Inevitably, however, where there are winners there have to be losers. The spelling test that ends with those pupils who did well holding up their hands reinforces the idea that school is like participating in a sporting event. It encourages pupils to work for themselves, taking no account of the performance of others except in the sense that they can be overtaken in the race to achieve educational success.

For some pupils this approach is undoubtedly highly motivating. They feel that they have a fair chance of success and are encouraged to do their best. Others learn over a period of time that their chances of success are minimal; they are always likely to be the losers. Consequently, they may elect to make less and less effort, or even to opt out. What schools teach them is that they are failures.

It was in response to this predominantly competitive ethos in many primary and secondary schools that the field of remedial education grew during the 1960s and 1970s. Recognising that some pupils were finding themselves regarded as failures, the case was made for some kind of positive discrimination. This has taken a number of different forms. Initially, the emphasis was on separate special classes or units with fewer pupils and a separate curriculum; more recently, the trend was towards withdrawal from ordinary lessons for short periods of intensive help in small groups; currently, the fashion is moving towards in-class support where an additional teacher or classroom assistant provides additional help to those pupils perceived as experiencing difficulties in learning.

It is possible to identify two common strands in these responses. First, there is an emphasis on developing a close working relationship between adult and child, in the belief that this is an effective way of creating the trust and confidence that is necessary in order that special help can be provided. Secondly, attention is given to analysing curriculum tasks and materials in such a way as to provide an individual response matched to the existing attainments and interests of the pupil.

There is much to be commended in these two lines of approach. Few would dispute that learning is likely to be enhanced if there is good rapport between teacher and pupils, and we have already emphasised the importance of paying attention to the match between pupils and tasks.

However, a number of areas of concern can result from an approach that places so much emphasis on making separate arrangements for particular pupils. It may mean that those who already have low self-esteem have their confidence further damaged by being confirmed as 'having a problem'. In addition the provision of periods of additional help may necessitate withdrawal from certain curriculum experiences. It is not uncommon to find pupils withdrawn for intensive work on so-called basic skills from lessons that include the sorts of activities that give learning purpose and meaning.

There are also potential difficulties associated with devising individual learning programmes for some pupils. Here, the idea is to design activities and materials carefully graded to take account of individual pupils' existing skills and knowledge, which will enable them to progress at their own rate. However, the removal of the pressure that is intended to be provided by competition may leave pupils with no other incentive for making an effort. This is perhaps why, so often in the past, work with remedial classes or groups has tended to be characterised by an air of complacency. Both teachers and pupils have no real sense of purpose or accountability that would help to maintain momentum.

Another problem with the idea of individual programmes is one to which we will be paying some greater attention later in this chapter. Put simply it is this: the emphasis that has been placed on planning around the needs of individual pupils has tended to lead to them spending long periods working in isolation. Consequently, they gain none of the academic or social benefits that can accrue from working collaboratively with their peers who have different aptitudes, interests and attitudes to learning.

Let us sum up what we have said so far. Providing individual attention to those pupils experiencing prolonged periods of difficulties in learning in the essentially competitive working ethos of many schools has a number of possible advantages. However, it also has some significant limitations, which result from the need to deal with the child separately. We will go on to argue that these call for a greater emphasis on forms of cooperative work in the classroom.

Cooperative learning

There are a number of significant arguments for an increase in the use of cooperative learning strategies in schools. These apply to all pupils.

It is important to recognise that we are not arguing for the abolition of other forms of task setting. There are occasions when competitive and individualised approaches will be appropriate. Indeed, it is important that children have opportunities to take part in different types of learning experiences in order that they can become more sensitive to, and aware of, their own preferences. Schools should be places where, as well as learning about 'things', they also learn about themselves as learners. This will only happen if pupils experience a wide range of tasks and activities presented in a variety of ways and have opportunities to reflect upon and interpret these encounters.

What are the major arguments for a greater emphasis on tasks and activities being set in ways that require pupils to work cooperatively? In particular, how might this encourage success in the classroom?

Learning is about taking risks. It requires us to take steps into the dark, trying something out when we are unsure about the outcome. Many people find it easier to take risks when they have the confidence that is often provided by sharing decisions and experiences with other people. So, for example, many people find that they are more likely to make an expensive purchase if they are out shopping with friends than if they are on their own. If this is so, it surely makes sense for pupils to be given opportunities to take risks in the classroom in collaboration with classmates who can provide support and encouragement.

Readers may well agree that many of their most significant learning experiences have occurred when they have been engaged in some encounter which required discussion, argument or problem-solving with others. Whilst listening silently to a lecture or reading privately can be an effective way of gathering information, for most of us significant ideas and leaps towards greater understanding of complex material are much more likely to occur when we have opportunities to think aloud, bouncing our thoughts off other people.

The area of personal and social development is recognised as an important theme within the curriculum by most teachers. We want to help our pupils to become more accomplished in living, working and playing in social contexts because this is the nature of the world into which we want them to be integrated. If much of school learning is carried out in a way that requires pupils to work in competition with one another or in isolation there is little opportunity for them to achieve objectives to do with these critical social areas. In classrooms where pupils are encouraged and helped to work cooperatively, however, they have opportunities to progress in these aspects of personal development whilst at the same time achieving their academic objectives.

On a more pragmatic level, an emphasis on cooperative learning can help pupils to become less dependent on their teachers. Pupils are encouraged to work collaboratively, supporting one another and seeking solutions to the problems presented by their tasks and activities. Where this works reasonably well (and it is by no means easy to achieve) it can give teachers time to concentrate on more important aspects of classroom life. Working arrangements in many classrooms, on the other hand, *encourage* pupils to be dependent on the teacher. This has the effect of burning up that most valuable educational resource, teacher time. The issue is perhaps summed up by the suggestion that schooling is the only business where the boss does all the work whilst the workers sit and watch!

There is one final, rather specific argument for a greater use of cooperative approaches. It relates to the need to integrate exceptional individuals into a new school or class. For the purposes of this analysis, 'exceptional' could refer to any pupil who is new to the scene. This might be a pupil who has moved into the area, possibly from another country; a child whose parent is in the armed forces; or a child from a traveller family. All such children find themselves having to fit into a new social context at the same time as they are adjusting to the demands of a curriculum which may be different from that of their previous school.

Similar problems are faced by pupils who have spent a period in a special school or unit. Currently efforts are being made to find ways of educating pupils with disabilities in mainstream primary and secondary schools. The main arguments for this are:

(1) Children must learn to live and work with all members of the community, whatever their disadvantages;

(2) Children who have personal disadvantages or disabilities are entitled to participate in a broad and balanced range of educational experiences;

(3) They should have the benefit of working and interacting with children who are perhaps more successful in learning.

It has to be said, however, that where such exceptional children become socially and intellectually isolated within mainstream classrooms, there are strong possibilities of negative outcomes resulting from their so-called integration. They may, for example, develop low self-esteem as a result of being stigmatised and stereotyped; learn to avoid challenging situations; suffer social rejection by other pupils; or be treated with paternalism. This being the case, we need to find ways of introducing them into a new class that encourage their success in both an academic and a social sense. We would suggest that a classroom in which there is a reasonable degree of cooperative working is more likely to help us achieve these goals.

In summary, then, the arguments that can be made for a greater emphasis on setting tasks and activities in such a way as to require cooperative learning include academic, social and organisational elements. As Johnson and Johnson (1986) argue, it is an approach that should be used 'whenever teachers want students to learn more, like school better, like each other better, have higher self-esteem, and learn more effective social skills'.

Given the strengths of the arguments for cooperative learning, it would be reasonable to assume that the use of such approaches would be widespread. What evidence there is, however, suggests that this is not the case.

In British primary schools, for example, there is an emphasis on the importance of discovery learning and problem-solving. Consequently it might be expected that teachers would make considerable use of approaches that require their pupils to work collaboratively on common tasks or activities. Evidence from observational research (e.g. Galton *et al.*, 1980) suggests that, whilst children are often seated in groups in primary classrooms, they are rarely asked to work in a collaborative manner.

Certainly in the special needs field, whether in mainstream or special schools, the emphasis that has been placed on planning for individuals has, as we have already suggested, tended to encourage organisational patterns in which pupils are required to work alone.

Perhaps somewhat surprisingly, the most encouraging area is secondary education where, as a result of a number of recent initiatives, including the development of new forms of recording and examination, there is some evidence of a growth of interest in more flexible approaches to learning (Hopkins, 1987). This impetus has been encouraged by various staff development programmes which have helped many secondary school teachers to understand the possible benefits of more active, participatory ways of working.

Staff development may be one important explanation why cooperative methods are not used to any great degree. It is probably true that very few of us have received any specific training in how to organise our classrooms in such a way as to facilitate effective group work. Consequently, we may lack the skills and confidence to try out ways of teaching that require us to take risks in front of that most critical of audiences, the class.

Here we must stress that, for cooperative methods of learning to be effective, they have to be planned, implemented and monitored very carefully. An ideological commitment to the idea is not enough and, indeed, can result in poorly conceived group activities which may quickly become a shambles. Whilst cooperative methods have an enormous potential for encouraging success in the classroom, this is unlikely to be the outcome unless they are used in a systematic and coordinated way.

For those wishing to consider introducing or extending their use of such approaches it is perhaps helpful to start by identifying some of the possible areas of difficulty. The following list of issues, adapted from Slavin (1983), provides a useful agenda for consideration:

○ How do we prevent one or two pupils doing all the work?
○ Why should pupils help each other to learn?
○ Why should they care what their classmates are doing?
○ How can we prevent the more successful pupils from belittling the contributions of others?
○ How can low-attaining pupils make a significant contribution?
○ How can group work be structured to facilitate the greatest possible learning for all members?
○ What kinds of materials and activities can be used?
○ How can we encourage colleagues to try cooperative methods?

Keeping these issues in mind we will now look at some of the essential features of cooperative learning.

Setting cooperative tasks

Arguably, the most important aspect of cooperative working must be an acceptance amongst members of a group that they can achieve their own objectives only if other members achieve theirs. The Johnsons refer to this as *positive interdependence*, the idea that 'one cannot succeed without the others'.

Positive interdependence may be achieved in different ways depending upon the nature of the set tasks, the content to be covered and the previous experience of the pupils. Here are some examples:

(1) Pupils may be required to work in pairs preparing a joint statement about a topic which they will be responsible for giving to a larger group.
(2) A group may be involved in a task that can only be completed if separate materials that are held by individual members are pooled.
(3) Individual members of a group may be assigned particular roles, e.g. chairperson, recorder, summariser, reporter.
(4) Each member may be asked to complete the first draft of a task that has to be completed by the whole group.
(5) A group may be told that they will be scored or graded as a result of the aggregate performance of work completed by individual members.

In setting up cooperative learning contexts, particularly with classes that are unfamiliar with this style of working, it makes sense to keep in mind the two critical aspects of teaching that were discussed earlier in this chapter. These are:

(1) ensuring pupils understand the nature and purpose of the activities in which they are engaged; and
(2) checking that tasks are matched to the existing attainments and interests of the pupils.

So, it is important to recognise that asking pupils to work collaboratively involves presenting them with new challenges. Effectively we are introducing an additional set of objectives to be achieved. As well as trying to achieve their academic objectives, they are being required to bear in mind objectives related to the skills of working in a group. Consequently, this aspect of the curriculum has to be planned and monitored as carefully as any other. This means, therefore, that the complexity and demands of working collaboratively should be introduced carefully and increased in a gradual fashion. Initially the difficulties should be minimised by, for example, simply asking each pupil to work with one familiar classmate on a straightforward task. The nature of the task demands, and group size and complexity, can be increased gradually as the pupils grow in competence and confidence.

Planning materials for cooperative learning

Where materials, particularly written materials of some kind, are to be used as part of group work, these must be carefully selected and presented. Here we have found the work of Lunzer *et al.* (1984) to be particularly helpful. They recommend a range of strategies for helping pupils to use reading more effectively across the curriculum.

Their approach is rooted in the view that reading should be seen as a strategy for learning. As such it involves decoding a text, making sense of what it is saying and relating this to the reader's existing understanding. By these processes judgements are made and knowledge is extended and modified. In other words, this is how learning takes place.

The essence of Lunzer and Gardner's work is a series of recommendations about how groups of pupils might work collaboratively to gain meaning from written materials. These involve pupils being taught particular strategies for analysing a text. So, for example, as part of a science or humanities lesson they might be asked to work with other pupils to:

(1) Locate and identify particular information in the material. This may involve underlining parts of the text to indicate where particular information can be found;
(2) Mark the located information in some way as an aid to understanding. Here sections of the text may be grouped into categories of particular significance;
(3) Organise the information and present it in a different form, perhaps by making a list of items located in the text or by filling in information on some form of table or graph.

Groups may also be asked to consider questions or issues that are not dealt with in the text or not dealt with adequately. This may well require them to think beyond the actual written material by considering questions such as, 'What might have happened if . . . ?', or 'What would be the result of . . . ?'

Other useful techniques recommended by Lunzer and Gardner involve some modifications of the texts to be used. For example:

(1) activities that involve the group in completing material that has words or sections deleted;
(2) the presentation of a text cut up into separate sentences or paragraphs that the group have to put into sequence; or
(3) prediction of likely outcomes before going on to read the next page or section.

It is important to note that all these approaches rely on the teacher providing effective explanations and, possibly, demonstrations of what the processes involve before groups are asked to start work.

It would be foolish to pretend that this type of approach to finding meaning in written material using group strategies solves the difficulties faced by those pupils who have limited reading skills. Our experience has been, however, that at the very least it can help them to participate in curriculum experiences from which they were previously excluded. As well, the experience of collaborating with more effective readers can be a means of helping them to recognise the potential usefulness and, indeed, enjoyment of reading.

Monitoring progress

The process of setting tasks and activities in ways that require pupils to cooperate needs to be monitored and reviewed carefully. Such monitoring should be carried out in relation to the two broad ranges of intended outcomes – those to do with academic progress and those concerned with the skills and attitudes necessary for working collaboratively with other pupils. The key issue is, are the pupils actively engaged in the tasks and activities that are set?

The two main strategies for monitoring classroom activity are observation and discussion. As the pupils are working, the teacher must move around the classroom collecting information through the use of questions and discussion. We need confirmation that all pupils understand what they are doing and why. And we need constantly to be checking that tasks and activities, and the objectives that underpin them, take adequate account of the existing skills and knowledge of each pupil.

Where necessary, further explanation may be given about the content of the activity or the working arrangements that have been agreed with the group. Attention should be paid to ensuring that specific guidelines for the group work are being applied and that individual members are contributing in the way that was intended. In particular, it is important to check that certain pupils are not dominating the proceedings and that others are not electing to opt out.

At the end of an activity or lesson the de-briefing of what has taken place is of crucial importance. Our experience is that this aspect of teaching is often poorly managed and sometimes completely ignored. If we think about the varied range of topics and experiences that pupils meet in a typical school day, we realise that it is essential that ways be found of helping them to draw out and record those that are significant.

De-briefing is a process of reviewing learning within which pupils are asked to consider what they have learned, what went well and what they may wish to remember in the future. It can be conducted in many different ways. For example, the teacher may simply review the activity or lesson with the whole class. Or, the pupils may talk in pairs or small groups, using the opportunity to think aloud about what they have achieved. Sometimes pupils may find it useful to keep some form of work journal in which they make entries describing their personal reactions and feelings about what they have been doing.

Whatever the methods used, the important feature of the de-briefing process is that it enables pupils to focus on their own learning and the contribution they have made to the activities that have taken place. It should be carried out in a positive climate, celebrating achievements and pointing to areas that might be developed during future activities.

Finally, it should be noted that once again this approach, as with most of those recommended in this book, assumes the existence of a collaborative working relationship between teachers and pupils. It is part of a wider aim to do with helping pupils to take responsibility for their own learning.

Summary

In making decisions about how tasks and activities are set we are seeking ways of helping pupils to be actively engaged in them. Effective teachers seem to achieve this by attempting to clarify the purpose and nature of what is planned, by seeking to match tasks and materials to individual pupils, by emphasising interest, and by providing support and feedback.

In many schools tasks and activities are often set in ways that require pupils to compete with one another. This means that some come to regard themselves as failures. The development of remedial education was an attempt to provide positive discrimination towards such pupils. This took a number of forms but tended to incorporate two common strands. These were an emphasis on a close working relationship between teachers and pupils, and the development of individualised programmes matched to the existing attainments and interest of the pupils. These approaches have a number of significant limitations, largely because of the emphasis on separating individual pupils from the broader context of the school curriculum.

When tasks and activities are set in ways that require pupils to work cooperatively, there is the possibility of a number of advantages which may be significant in helping all pupils to experience classroom success. These can only be achieved, however, if such approaches are planned, implemented and monitored carefully.

Recommended further reading

Bennet, N., Desforges, C., Cockburn, A. and Wilkinson, B. (1984). *The Quality of Pupil Learning Experiences*. London: Lawrence Erlbaum.
Based on observations of primary school teachers, this book provides some helpful suggestions about the difficult issue of task setting.

Galton, M. and Simon, B. (eds) (1980). *Progress and Performance in the Primary Classroom*. London: RKP.
One of a series of books on primary practice that resulted from the research project 'ORACLE'. Argues that many pupils in primary schools never experience cooperative group work at all.

Johnson, D. W. and Johnson, R. T. (1986). Mainstreaming and co-operative learning strategies. *Exceptional Children*, **52**, 6, 553–561.
An account of the essential elements of cooperative learning approaches and how they can be used. Provides a list of excellent references for those who wish to pursue this topic.

Lunzer, E., Gardner, K., Davies, F. and Green, T. (1984). *Learning from the Written Word*. Edinburgh: Oliver and Boyd.
An excellent source book of ideas and examples of how to encourage pupils to learn more effectively from written texts across the curriculum.

Schniedewind, N. and Salend, S. J. (1987). Cooperative learning works. *Teaching Exceptional Children*, **19**, 2, 22–25.
A short, readable account of how to use cooperative learning approaches.

Slavin, R. E. (1983). *Co-operative Learning*. London: Longman.
A summary of hundreds of studies supporting the effectiveness of non-competitive learning.

Topping, K. (1988). *The Peer Tutoring Handbook*. London: Croom Helm.
A useful introduction to the idea of peer tutoring, an approach to cooperative learning that has become popular recently.

CHAPTER 5

Classroom Arrangements

We have discussed the issues and ideas presented in this book with many teachers in recent years, including those who have attended courses and workshops in which we have participated. In general, the response has been positive despite the fact that certain of our themes leave a question mark over some current practice.

Certainly teachers we meet agree that we should be seeking ways of working that encourage success in the classroom for all pupils. They also agree that it makes sense to plan and monitor the implementation of the curriculum in order to take account of individual pupils and ensure understanding of what is intended. The big problem, about which we are regularly reminded, is one of *time*. How does a busy teacher find the time to do all the things that we are proposing?

There are no easy answers to this age-old issue. What we recommend is that all of us should try to learn from our own experience of teaching and share our knowledge with colleagues.

In the British context, classrooms have tended to be surrounded by secrecy, with the rights of individual teachers to work in their own way carefully protected. Few teachers get regular opportunities to observe their colleagues working and relatively little in-service attention has been given to matters of classroom organisation. The methods of teaching and learning upon which most of us base our practice are rooted in our experience as children in school and the outcomes of the trial and error of our efforts in the classroom.

This is not to say that trial and error is of no importance. Central to the position taken throughout this book is the view that the most important source of learning is personal experience. We learn from what we do. However, experience has to be analysed and interpreted if significant learning is to take place.

This, then, is the focus of the chapter. It addresses the question:

How do we make effective use of the
resources available to facilitate learning?

We assume that the two most important resources for learning in the classroom are the teacher and the pupils themselves. Learning is best facilitated if all these human resources are able to interact in positive ways. The key management task is to encourage such interactions. Our emphasis is thus on finding ways of managing the classroom that increase the time available for teaching – as opposed to carrying out routine organisational tasks.

Our decisions in the area of classroom organisation should be influenced by the two key factors which also dominated our discussions in Chapters 3 and 4. These are: seeking to ensure that pupils understand our decisions, and taking account of the skills and knowledge that pupils bring to the classroom.

What is provided in this chapter is a discussion of some of the key issues involved in making decisions about classroom arrangements. This is presented not as a set of prescriptions on how to teach, but rather as an agenda for reviewing practice. We hope it will be used as a basis for pinpointing areas of practice that may be worthy of development.

The sources of the content of the chapter are our own experience of teaching, of observing teaching and of talking with teachers about their teaching. These sources have been shaped and enriched by some of the recent research evidence about the strategies used by effective teachers (e.g. Brophy, 1983; Rosenshine, 1983).

Aspects of decision-making

We will examine the day-to-day decisions faced by teachers in terms of the following three key aspects of their work:

(1) providing explanations
(2) keeping pupils busy
(3) reviewing learning.

These three aspects of decision-making are usually dealt with in an interactive way. For purposes of analysis and reflection, however, examining them independently helps us to look at some of the demands that are made on teacher and pupil time, and provides a useful framework for considering how priorities about the use of time should be established.

(1) Providing explanations

In our experience, successful teachers find time to provide their pupils with explanations about the nature of the topics under discussion or the activities being undertaken. They may choose to do this in a variety of ways. However, a common feature seems to be an emphasis on explanations that help pupils to understand the nature and purpose of the work which they are doing.

Throughout this and the previous two chapters we emphasise the importance of pupils' understanding. As far as the age of the pupils permits, therefore, we are suggesting that they should understand: (a) *what* they are trying to do, i.e. their learning objectives; (b) *how* they are trying to do it, i.e. the nature of their tasks and activities; and (c) how the classroom is organised so that they can engage in those activities. Learning difficulties can quite easily be created when insufficient time and attention are given to explaining our decisions in any one of these three areas.

Sometimes one of the unintended outcomes of attempts to organise classrooms in a more flexible way, with a greater emphasis on pupils working on individualised assignments, is that the teacher has less time to give pupils explanations at the outset of particular activities. Too often the key instruction seems to be, 'Carry on with the work you were doing yesterday'. As a consequence the pupils may be engaged in completing exercises that have little or no purpose or meaning.

The important features of explanations, whatever form they take, are that they should:

○ take account of the pupils' existing skills and knowledge;
○ help pupils to relate new learning to previous experience;
○ help clarify the purpose of particular tasks or activities.

The most obvious format is that of the presentation given by the teacher at the outset of an activity or lesson. The art of making such presentations in a clear and interesting way is an important part of any teacher's repertoire, and its importance should not be underestimated in our enthusiasm for more active methods of learning. Similarly, the use of questioning remains an excellent strategy for drawing out the pupils' earlier learning or personal experience as starting points for further discussions. Having said that, we need to be wary of the danger of the classroom becoming dominated by teacher talk. Picking up some of the themes of earlier chapters, we would want to encourage the active involvement of pupils in making their own explanations of what a theme or topic involves.

Once again this can take a variety of forms. For example, instead of the teacher questioning the pupils, pupils may question one another as a result of an introductory presentation by the teacher or as a result of some initial reading. Pupils might also be asked to work in pairs or groups to formulate key questions to be put to the teacher.

Where pupils are required to search for explanations from written material, it is important to help them to develop suitable study skills. The approaches to text analysis referred to in Chapter 4 are useful in this respect. Another helpful strategy recommended by Lunzer and Gardner (1979) is known as *SQ3R*. It involves teaching pupils how to:

○ **Survey**
An initial rapid sampling of the material to stimulate interest and give a sense of direction to subsequent intensive reading.
○ **Question**
At the same time as this initial contact, questions are formulated which are intended to promote anticipation of and prediction from the material to be read.
○ **Read**
Having surveyed the material and discussed questions raised, detailed reading should be an active search rather than a passive read.
○ **Review**
This involves organising and reviewing what has been learned from the text and taking steps to prevent forgetting.
○ **Recite**
Finally the content is recited in order to demonstrate understanding.

This approach lends itself to collaborative group work and can be particularly useful in helping pupils who lack confidence in their reading to find meaning from difficult material.

A benefit of involving pupils actively in determining their own explanations of particular topics is that this is a means of checking their interpretations and understanding before proceeding. These may be quite different from those intended by the teacher and, of course, may lead to misunderstandings.

This brings us to the issue of the difficulty level of explanations. A number of research projects (e.g. Bennett *et al.*, 1984) suggest that one of the major difficulties teachers experience is in setting and presenting tasks at an appropriate level, given the diversity of experience and attainments within any class. The art is to know how far to go forward in increasing the level of difficulty whilst at the same time ensuring that all the pupils in a class or group will be able to cope with the demands made. Explanations which pupils perceive as being too complex are likely to discourage concentration, particularly amongst those who have a negative view of themselves as learners. Equally, there is little value if pupils do not experience the stimulation that comes from being challenged.

(2) Keeping pupils busy

The problem of how to use available time becomes even more acute when members of a class are working independently or are engaged in some form of group activity. If explanations have been successfully provided and necessary resources made available the teacher should have some time to give to individual pupils. On the other hand, where explanations have been inadequate, or resources are unavailable, management difficulties are prone to arise. For example, discipline problems often occur in such classes.

What other areas of decision-making are significant in terms of keeping pupils actively engaged in the tasks and activities set? The work of Kounin (1970) is particularly relevant in this respect. As a result of his research, he traced relationships between the behaviour of teachers and pupils' involvement in their work, coming to the conclusion that four areas are particularly critical.

Kounin defines these using his own somewhat idiosyncratic terminology. First of all, he notes the need for teacher 'with-it-ness'. That is the skill of knowing what is happening around the classroom and making pupils aware of his or her presence. Secondly, he refers to 'overlappingness', an ability to attend to more than one thing at a time. This may mean, for example, monitoring events going on in a different part of the room whilst giving attention to one pupil or group of pupils. The third important teacher behaviour is 'momentum'. This involves keeping up the pace of learning while managing the orderly change of activities or movement about the classroom. Finally, Kounin also sees what he refers to as 'group alerting' as being important. This means keeping pupils involved by holding them accountable for their work and participation. This may be achieved by keeping them in suspense; making them feel that something new or exciting might happen at any time; or making them conscious that at any moment they might be called on to make a contribution.

Kounin's work also suggests that pupils tend to be less engaged when they are asked to work independently. He goes on to make various recommendations which are in line with some of the suggestions made in this book. For example, he argues that the interest value of assigned tasks will have a positive influence on the degree of attention pupils give. In addition, he recommends that work should be at the right level of difficulty – easy enough to allow successful completion but difficult enough to challenge each pupil.

Teacher movement around the classroom during periods where pupils are involved in working independently can also have an effect on pupil attention. A teacher on a course recently spent some time observing a child in a primary school who was said to 'have learning difficulties'. Somewhat to her surprise she found her attention wandering away from the pupil towards the teacher, who rarely left his seat at the front of the class. Instead, children came to him to receive help or have their books marked. As far as she could see, all these interactions were initiated by the pupils. This state of affairs was in some senses commendable in that the children were being required to take responsibility for their own work. However, observations over two subsequent mornings indicated that a child might have little or no contact with the teacher if he or she chose not to seek it. Indeed, the child under observation busied himself at the far end of the room, never bothering the teacher or being bothered by him.

This rather extreme example points to the need for us to be sensitive to our movements in the class and their likely impact on the progress of individual pupils. Certainly, where pupils are working alone or in groups, we need to be moving about the room, encouraging and praising the pupils' efforts, and providing feedback and further explanations as necessary. It makes sense, also, to make such encounters as brief as possible in order that work is not interrupted and that teacher attention can be shared around all members of the class. If it is found that a lot of time is having to be spent in re-explaining points to individual pupils, this is probably an indication that the initial explanations were in some way inadequate.

The use of praise as a means of encouraging children's efforts is another important aspect of teacher behaviour. Recent years have seen considerable attention in books and on in-service courses to teacher praise as a strategy for keeping pupils busy and helping them to succeed in their learning. At times this emphasis has appeared to be based on an almost blind faith that simply increasing the amount of praise used by a teacher will improve children's academic progress and social behaviour.

The issue is much more complex than this, although it is the case that teachers' optimism tends to be reflected in their pupils' achievements. Brophy (1983) has reviewed the extensive research evidence about the use of praise in the classroom and provides some helpful suggestions. He recommends that teachers should concentrate on praising well rather than on praising often. The danger is that praise may be given in ways that reduce the extent to which pupils find working on, or completing, their tasks intrinsically rewarding. To avoid this, care should be taken to give praise only for genuine progress or accomplishment, particularly in cases where pupils do not realise or fully appreciate their achievements. The main aim must be to encourage pupils to expend effort because they find enjoyment and satisfaction in learning.

(3) Reviewing learning

Throughout this book we emphasise the importance of monitoring pupil learning. This is one of the noticeable skills of successful teachers. We also wish to encourage the idea that pupils can be helped to take some responsibility for reviewing their own learning experiences.

In some aspects of the curriculum the very nature of the tasks leads pupils to take responsibility for monitoring their own progress by keeping some form of written record. For instance, certain commercial mathematics schemes require pupils to keep a note of assignment cards completed. Another example, involving a more qualitative approach, is when teachers ask pupils to write reviews of the books they have read including some evaluative comments.

A strategy we find useful is to get pupils working in pairs or small groups at the end of an activity or, indeed, at the end of the day, talking about what they have been doing. We suggest that they think about what they have enjoyed, what they have achieved, what has been important and how they feel about it.

When we recommend this way of working to teachers some are rather sceptical, suggesting that their pupils would not be able or willing to take part in such activities. Our experience is that, if pupils (even quite young children) are given guidance and encouragement, they will become very actively involved in this form of self-review, often surprising their teachers by their understanding and sensitivity.

We think particularly of one primary school where this approach is introduced during the children's first few months in school. Consequently they grow up through the school with the expectation that they will be required to be involved in regular sessions of reflection and self-review. So, by the time they reach the age of 11, they have become skilful in this aspect of their school life and used to the idea that they should share responsibility for their own progress. A sad postscript to this story is that many of the same pupils, when they transfer to the local secondary school, lose their feelings of confidence and independence as a result of being dealt with by teachers who prefer to keep all the responsibility themselves.

One final point is worth noting at this stage – the need for us as teachers to review what we have learned about teaching and learning as a result of particular activities or lessons. We are seeking to encourage teachers to be sensitive to themselves as learners in the classroom alongside their pupils, using the same idea of reflecting on experience.

Finding the time

What then are the messages that emerge from this discussion of some of the ways in which effective teachers arrange their classrooms in order to provide explanations, keep their pupils busy, and review learning? What are the ways in which they find some time to carry out these key aspects of their work?

The first thing to say is that simply recognising that these are key aspects is an important step forward. Organising the classroom, planning activities and dealing with all the unexpected events that occur can take up so much energy and time that little is left for helping pupils achieve success in their learning. Issues of organisation can become ends in themselves rather than means to more important ends.

A second point is that classroom arrangements that facilitate greater pupil involvement can be a useful means of releasing the teacher to carry out more significant duties. This does not mean that teachers lose control over what happens in their classrooms. Indeed, it is probably only possible in situations where the teacher's influence is so well established that he or she has the confidence to delegate responsibility to members of the class.

Finally we must repeat once again our view that all of this necessitates an attitude of mind amongst teachers of wanting to learn from experience, of seeking to develop, from an examination of their own practice, new solutions to old problems.

Support in the classroom

The bulk of this chapter has concentrated on what we consider to be the two main resources for learning in any classroom – the teacher and the pupils themselves. The aim is to manage arrangements in ways that allow the maximum time possible to be concentrated on interactions that will encourage success in the classroom.

Another possible resource may be available, that of additional people who are able to spend some time helping in the classroom. These may be pupils acting as peer tutors to younger children; parents who have volunteered to give up some of their spare time; classroom assistants assigned to individual pupils deemed to have special educational needs; or, as is increasingly the trend in secondary education, teachers who formerly worked with small withdrawal groups who are now expected to provide in-class support teaching.

The existence of any additional help is clearly of potential benefit, not least in arranging the classroom in ways that take more account of pupils as individuals. It can simply provide a little more of that precious commodity, time. However, additional help can create additional difficulties. Let us look at some of the possibilities.

First, it can have negative effects on learning outcomes. For example, situations can arise where the presence of a classroom helper of some kind means that certain pupils are helped to complete their assignments without fully understanding what they involve or facing the problems they pose. Consequently little or no significant learning may take place. The helper may also be a source of distraction, with pupils being interrupted as they attempt to carry out their tasks. One of us recently overheard a teenage girl in a science lesson express her irritation at the presence of a support teacher by saying, 'If you would just leave us alone we would be able to get on with our work'.

Support in the classroom can also have damaging effects on attitudes. Pupils identified in front of their classmates as 'needing special help' may well feel distressed. They might also develop a sense of dependence on their helper, feeling little or no need to cooperate with other pupils in the class. It may also be the case that the teacher in charge of the class feels that there is no need to take responsibility for those children who have the benefit of outside support.

Our greatest concern about the presence of some form of additional help in the classroom, however, is that this may serve to maintain the status quo. One of the positive roles of pupils who experience difficulties is to give the teacher some feedback that decisions that have been made about objectives, tasks and activities, or classroom arrangements are in some sense inappropriate for at least some members of the class. If such difficulties are masked by the intervention of other adults who occupy the pupils' attention, or help them complete their assigned tasks, the teacher may be prevented from becoming aware of significant information that could be used to improve the way the class is conducted.

How might these difficulties be avoided? How can we gain the full benefits of any extra help that is available? In general terms the way forward is to aim for a cooperative working arrangement, where both adults in a classroom have an agreement as to how it is to operate, what their aims are and what roles each will play. All of this takes time. Time is needed beforehand for planning and, indeed, afterwards in order to reflect on and learn from the experience of working together. When it works well, a major benefit of any cooperative teaching arrangement is the professional stimulation that occurs as a result of sharing ideas and evaluating outcomes with a colleague.

Thomas (1986) reports some interesting attempts to find ways in which the presence of more than one adult in the classroom might be used to best effect, particularly in responding to those pupils experiencing some difficulties in learning. He suggests that the aim should be to ensure that all members of a class are actively engaged in the tasks set by the teacher whilst at the same time providing the maximum amount of help possible to individual pupils.

One particular strategy he recommends is known as 'room management'. It was developed originally for use by personnel working with children and adults who have severe learning difficulties. The basic idea is that adults working in a cooperative setting are assigned specific roles during what is referred to as the 'activity period' – a specific period of time, usually of about one hour. The roles are as follows:

individual helper – is responsible for taking individual or small groups of pupils for short periods of intensive help.

activity manager – attempts to keep the rest of the class involved in the tasks and activities that have been set.

mover – aims to maintain the flow of activity by dealing with matters relating to resources. In a well-organised class these duties are usually delegated to the pupils.

Evidence from work in primary schools suggests that children's rate of engagement in the tasks that have been set can be increased by up to 30 per cent as a result of using this type of room management strategy.

Reviewing classroom arrangements

Implicit in our discussion of classroom arrangements, of course, is the need to keep decisions under review. This is the only way in which the flexibility we are seeking can be achieved. Throughout, our aim is to see that the resources that are available – human and material – are used to facilitate learning.

In reviewing classroom arrangements we must once again return to our two pervading themes, the need for pupil understanding and the importance of taking account of pupils' existing attainments. Bearing these in mind, we should seek ways of helping members of a class to understand how the room is to be organised, the way resources are to be managed, and what to do if things go wrong. Then they should be made aware that they have the right to comment on these arrangements. Effectively they are being invited to share responsibility for the ongoing evaluation and development of their own learning environment. In so doing they are also having opportunities to manipulate aspects of that environment in ways that take account of their own preferences.

Summary

Decisions about classroom arrangements are to a large degree about time. They are concerned with the use of time by the two major resources for learning in any classroom, the teacher and the pupils themselves. Emphasis needs to be given to increasing the amount of time available for pupils and teachers to interact in ways that facilitate learning.

In considering their use of time, teachers should keep in mind the following key aspects of their work: providing explanations, keeping pupils busy, and reviewing learning. Improvements in practice in these areas are likely to be achieved by reflecting on personal experience and sharing ideas with colleagues.

One significant way of finding time to help pupils with their tasks and activities is to share with them responsibility for making decisions about classroom arrangements. Another possibility is the provision of various forms of additional support, although this can have negative effects if poorly planned.

Finally, it is important that decisions about classroom arrangements are kept under review.

Recommended further reading

Anderson, L. W. (ed.) (1984). *Time and School Learning*. London: Croom Helm.
The contributors to this book examine the concept of teaching as the management of attention over time.

Brophy, J. E. (1983). Classroom organisation and management. *The Elementary School Journal* **83**, 4, 264–285.
A very useful review article of recent research evidence about classroom organisation.

Kounin, J. (1970). *Discipline and Group Management in Classrooms*. New York: Holt, Rinehart & Winston.
An account of Kounin's much-quoted research designed to find out about group management techniques applicable to classroom situations. He concludes that effective group management enables teachers to give more attention to the needs of individual pupils.

Robertson, J. (1981). *Effective Classroom Control*. London: Hodder & Stoughton.
A useful companion to Kounin's work, providing some practical suggestions on classroom management.

Rosenshine, B. (1983). Teacher functions in instructional programmes. *The Elementary School Journal*, **83**, 4, 335–351.
Summarises research findings about successful teaching. Whilst it provides a useful source of ideas, the focus of attention is on the achievement of a narrow range of learning outcomes.

Wragg, E. C. (ed.) (1984). *Classroom Teaching Skills*. London: Croom Helm.
Contains some useful accounts of research findings about teachers who are effective classroom managers.

CHAPTER 6

Summary and Implications

In this final chapter we summarise the central message of this book and consider the implications for the education service in general.

Central message

Much of the thinking of those who work in the education service is dominated by an acceptance of the assumption that a proportion of pupils in school have something wrong with them – they have learning difficulties. Consequently, in an attempt to provide various forms of positive discrimination for these pupils, a separate wing of the service has developed, made up of teachers and other professional groups who are seen as having specialist expertise in dealing with learning difficulties. Some of these work as members of staff of particular schools, whilst others adopt a peripatetic role between schools.

Despite the undoubted good intentions of those involved in setting up and carrying out this work, a negative outcome has been that many teachers in primary and secondary schools have developed the view that they are incapable of dealing with those youngsters who are seen as being special. Moreover, the difficulties of these pupils have tended to be analysed in isolation, thus distracting attention from a whole range of factors that might have significance in helping them to learn.

This being so, we recommend an approach to teaching and learning that recognises that all of us experience difficulties with certain tasks, and, indeed, that learning difficulties are associated with the attempt of individuals to carry out particular activities. In other words, learning difficulties are context bound.

In seeking ways of helping all pupils to experience success in the classroom we should focus our attention on those factors over which we have a significant influence, particularly those classroom factors associated with the planning and implementation of the curriculum. Our aim as teachers must be to improve our own practice, particularly by taking account of the individuality of pupils within our classes and finding ways to help pupils to understand the nature and purpose of the tasks and activities in which they are engaged.

Our suggested framework for improving practice is based on the belief that all of us learn most from our own experience. Consequently we want to encourage the idea of teachers reflecting upon and interpreting their work in the classroom. To facilitate them we need an approach to assessment that monitors the outcomes of decisions about the curriculum. This approach, which we prefer to call classroom evaluation, involves the continuous monitoring of decisions about objectives, tasks and activities, and classroom arrangements.

Implications

A number of important implications arise from this line of argument. They need to be considered by all those involved in providing education: politicians, administrators, inspectors, parents, head teachers and, of course, teachers in all types of schools. These implications can be summarised as four brief statements. They are:

○ Individual needs, not special needs
○ Entitlement, not exclusion
○ Flexibility, not rigidity
○ Support, not experts.

These statements are interdependent. An examination of each tends to lead to the next.

Individual needs, not special needs

As a result of the 1981 Education Act, the categories of handicap that had previously been the administrative basis for special education in Britain were abolished. These were replaced by the concept of special educational need. In the period that followed this legislation the term 'pupil with special educational need' quickly became fashionable in primary and secondary schools, where it has generally replaced terms such as 'remedial' or 'slow learner'.

On the face of it the term 'special educational need' is an attractive one. It seems to focus attention on individual children, indicating that something particular and positive should be arranged to meet their needs. Unfortunately it has gradually acquired a definition that is less optimistic. It has simply become a more polite way of referring to pupils who are seen as being inadequate. Even worse, it tends to be used as a 'catch-all' phrase for any pupils who are not getting on well with their work.

The fear expressed by Tomlinson (1982) that the legislation might lead to the labelling and segregation of a greater proportion of pupils is unfortunately coming true. Indeed the idea, referred to in the Warnock Report, that 20 per cent of pupils will experience difficulties of one kind or another at some stage in their school career has gained a new meaning. Instead of an estimate to inform our thinking, it has become a target. As in the past, attempts are being made to identify a group of pupils who have special needs in order that special provision can be made for them. This means drawing 'a line' across the pupils in a school in order to designate the 'bottom 20 per cent'.

This strategy of identifying and labelling a sub-group of pupils as needing special attention is in one sense understandable. An examination of the history of education indicates that it is a proven way of winning or preserving additional resources. For example, early special schools for the blind and the deaf were introduced as a result of campaigns mounted around simple labels which could be used to draw the attention, sympathy and donations of members of the general public. Similarly, today it is not uncommon to hear of head teachers appealing to local education authorities not to withdraw staff since this would damage provision for special needs. In addition, the strategy continues to be used by groups wishing to establish provision for children said to be 'dyslexic', 'autistic' or 'gifted'.

However, what we must learn from history is that this tactic for gaining resources is often used at considerable cost. It becomes a form of stereotyping, involving generalisations about a group of individuals based upon a small number of shared characteristics. The outcome is almost inevitable: the individuals are perceived as being similar and are treated accordingly.

We recommend, therefore, that all of us in the education service should seek to eradicate the use of all forms of labels, including the now fashionable 'special needs', recognising that they are essentially discriminatory. Instead we should find ways of acknowledging the individuality of each pupil, that all children experience learning difficulties and that all can experience success. The aim must be to organise schools in ways that help teachers to respond to and, indeed, celebrate the personal qualities and interests of each member of their class. The achievement of this would be to the benefit of all pupils.

Entitlement, not exclusion

Responding to pupils as individuals does not mean that we should ignore the relationship each has with the wider social context in which he or she exists. A role of schools has to be to prepare young people to understand and accept their responsibilities as members of their community. Consequently they must learn that, whilst their individuality is respected and preferences encouraged, this occurs within constraints and guidelines that are there in order to protect the rights of others in the community of which they are a part.

In terms of the broad purposes and framework of the curriculum, all pupils should be entitled to participate in a common range of experiences. This is necessary not only in order that they can learn about their roles and responsibilities in the community at large, but also because in a democracy this is surely their right.

The current debate about the British government's proposals to introduce a National Curriculum clearly has implications for this issue. On the positive side it is in sympathy with what we are suggesting – it is an intention to provide all pupils with an entitlement to a broad education. Our concern, as is that of many teachers, is with some of the detailed proposals. First of all there is the fear that the idea of a broad curriculum for all pupils may be lost if the guidelines and programmes of study that are developed are narrow in concept. This possibility seems to be even more likely if the proposal to introduce attainment targets and regular testing of all pupils involves the use of narrowly conceived assessment procedures. There is little doubt that tests and examinations influence classroom practice and that narrow forms of assessment are likely to lead to a restricted and, indeed, restricting curriculum.

A further worry, which relates to our earlier comments about the problems associated with the concept of special educational need, is that forms of assessment that identify certain pupils as failures will lead to the process of writing Statements of Special Educational Need becoming a frequently used means of excluding pupils from the requirement to participate in the National Curriculum. Those who are said to have something wrong, some learning difficulty, may be offered a separate form of curriculum more suited to their needs. Thus their entitlement to a broad curriculum will be withdrawn on the basis that this is in their best interests.

So, whatever the source of the framework of the curriculum – whether this is agreed nationally, as seems likely, locally or within individual schools – we would urge those involved in the decision-making process to commit themselves to providing a broad and common range of curriculum experiences for *all* pupils.

Flexibility, not rigidity

How then do these statements about the need for an emphasis on individuality and the entitlement of all pupils to a broad curriculum fit together?

A theme that permeates this book is the need for flexibility. Essentially we are arguing that, within whatever curriculum guidelines exist, classrooms have to be managed in ways that enable teachers to respond to pupils as individuals as they encounter the tasks and activities that are set. Nowhere is it argued that this is easy. It represents the very essence of the pressures faced by most teachers.

The ways in which schools are organised can, however, help teachers as they seek to improve their professional competence in this respect. In particular, the way in which pupils are grouped into classes can have a significant effect. There is, we believe, a need to move away from systems of grouping that are so rigid as to undermine attempts to respond to the individuality of pupils. This means the rejection of systems such as streaming or banding, or the creation of special classes for low attainers, all strategies that place pupils together in the belief that they have a shared potential for learning. These are administrative systems introduced largely for the benefit of adults which almost always work to the disadvantage of pupils.

Allocation of pupils into this form of ability grouping is often based on data gathered as a result of forms of assessment that give preconceived answers to preconceived questions. Once again they lead us into the trap of making generalisations about groups of pupils (e.g. 'This is the high-flying group'), which in turn leads us to form stereotypes in our minds and distracts attention from the particular qualities of individuals. They also run the risk of promoting self-fulfilling prophecy, whereby pupils live up to or, more often, down to the expectations we appear to have of what they might achieve.

Consequently schools should seek to group pupils in ways that take

account of their unique range of attainments, interests and preferences, avoiding at all costs rigid systems that force pupils to fit into pre-
determined adult stereotypes of what they are like.

Support, not experts

Most of what we have to say is aimed at teachers. What they choose to
do, what they feel capable of doing, what happens between them and
their pupils in the classroom, are the most critical aspects of the work
of any school. Those in the background, the managers of the school
system, must therefore see it as their key role to organise schools in
ways that give maximum support to teachers as they attempt to teach
in the flexible and responsive way that we recommend. This means that
their decisions and style of management should encourage teachers to
be confident in their ability to teach all their pupils successfully.

So much of what has gone on in the past has had the opposite effect.
The emphasis on identifying groups of children as being special has
undermined the confidence of many teachers, encouraging them to
take the view that these pupils are outside their professional scope.
Similarly the presence of designated experts has reinforced the idea
that what is required are specialist teaching techniques which cannot
be used by most teachers.

Many of those who have come to be regarded as experts in the
special needs field (and the authors of this book are striking examples
of this) have done very well out of encouraging this type of thinking.
Our careers have developed very successfully as a result of the widespread belief that we are able to use techniques that are not generally
available. This leads us to a point of some discomfort. If we are promoting an approach to teaching and learning that rejects as harmful
the idea of experts, what happens to those of us who have hitherto
fulfilled such roles?

In general what we have to do is to give up approaches that concentrate our efforts on devising specialist teaching methods for small
groups of pupils whom we have identified as being in some way different from their peers. Our efforts should be focused not on making
separate arrangements but on helping to make all teaching more effective for all pupils.

This means that such additional teaching resources as are available
should be geared towards helping all teachers to organise the learning
environment in ways that allow flexibility to respond to pupils as individuals. They should be used to help in the planning, implementation

and evaluation of teaching procedures that make effective use of the presence of more than one adult in the classroom. Effective use, that is, in terms of facilitating pupil learning, but also with respect to the professional development of those involved. Where two teachers are able to work together effectively this provides an excellent opportunity for both to improve their practice through a process of collaborative classroom evaluation in the spirit of what is recommended in Chapter 2.

If teachers are to work in the ways that are recommended in this book, they must have the support of those around them. The process of change is about learning to do new things; just as pupils need support as they learn, so do teachers. A task of management must be to help create a climate in school in which teachers feel confident to try new ways of working. What is required is an atmosphere in which individual teachers feel supported and respected as they make efforts to learn about themselves as teachers. Indeed, we should go so far as to suggest that, in schools where teachers feel recognised for the individual contributions they make, they are more likely to respond positively to the individual contributions of their pupils.

It is important also to recognise that change in education is almost always a process not an event. It happens, if it happens at all, as a result of those involved seeking to achieve a personal interpretation of what is involved and then implementing the change in their own ways. Michael Fullan (1982), who has written so eloquently about processes of change in schools, refers to it as 'the science of muddling through'. It takes time, it is often complex, it can lead to ambiguity, and it requires those involved to take risks before that most difficult and demanding of audiences, the class.

A final point

Whilst most of what is said in this chapter has an eye to a wider readership, the most important readers at whom this book is aimed are teachers. We hope you have found our ideas relevant and meaningful. More than anything else we hope you are convinced by our argument that your most important source of professional improvement is your own practice. Try to learn from and with your pupils.

Summary

The arguments that are presented in this book have important implications for the way in which the education service is organised and managed. Broadly what is proposed is a greater emphasis on:

- ○ individual needs, not special needs;
- ○ entitlement, not exclusion;
- ○ flexibility, not rigidity;
- ○ support, not experts.

Recommended further reading

Booth, T., Potts, P. and Swann, W. (eds) (1987). *Preventing Difficulties in Learning*. Oxford: Blackwell.
Includes some useful accounts of teachers' attempts to make classroom practice more flexible in response to pupils' individuality.

Dessent, T. (1987). *Making the Ordinary School Special*. London: Falmer.
The author, an educational psychologist, argues that pupils do not need an army of outside experts dealing with individual pupils for whom schools are inadequately resourced or organised.

Fullan, M. (1982). *The Meaning of Educational Change*. New York: Teachers College Press.
Essential reading for anybody interested in how schools can improve.

Golby, M. and Gulliver, J. R. (1985). Whose remedies, whose ills? A critical review of remedial education, in C. J. Smith (ed.), *New Directions in Remedial Education*. London: Falmer.
Originally published in 1979, this hard-hitting paper describes remedial teachers as ambulance men picking up the casualties of an inappropriate curriculum.

Postman, N. and Weingartner, C. (1969). *Teaching as a Subversive Activity*. London: Penguin.
Almost 20 years on, this polemic still has important messages for teachers about the importance of helping pupils to learn how to learn.

Purkey, S. C. and Smith, M. S. (1983). Effective schools: A review. *The Elementary School Journal*. **83**, 4, 426–452.
Whilst being critical of recent literature on school effectiveness, this extensive review article concludes that many of the findings of this research are worthy of serious consideration.

Reid, K., Hopkins, D. and Holly, P. (1987). *Towards the Effective School*. Oxford: Blackwell.
This book offers a survey of recent research into effective schooling and offers some suggestions for improving practice.

References

Ainscow, M. and Tweddle, D. A. (1979). *Preventing Classroom Failure: An Objectives Approach*, London: David Fulton Publishers.

Ainscow, M. and Tweddle, D. A. (1984). *Early Learning Skills Analysis*, Chichester: London: David Fulton Publishers.

Barrow, R. (1984). *Giving Teaching Back to Teachers*, Brighton: Wheatsheaf.

Bennett, N., Desforges, C., Cockburn, A. and Wilkinson, B. (1984). *The Quality of Pupil Learning Experiences*, London: Lawrence Erlbaum.

Brennan, W. K. (1974). *Shaping the Education of Slow Learners*, London: Routledge & Kegan Paul.

Broadfoot, P. (ed.) (1986). *Profiles and Records of Achievement*, London: Holt, Rinehart & Winston.

Brophy, J. E. (1983). Classroom organisation and management, *The Elementary School Journal*, **83** (4), 264–285.

Fullan, M. (1982). *The Meaning of Educational Change*, New York: Teachers College Press.

Galton, M. and Simon, B. (eds) (1980). *Progress and Performance in the Primary School*, London: Routledge & Kegan Paul.

Holt, J. (1964). *How Children Fail*, London: Penguin.

Hopkins, D. (1987). The new initiatives: An overview, *British Journal of Special Education*, **14** (4), 137–140.

Johnson, D. W. and Johnson, R. T. (1986). Mainstreaming and co-operative learning strategies, *Exceptional Children*, **52** (6), 553–561.

Kounin, J. (1970). *Discipline and Group Management in Classrooms*, New York: Holt, Rinehart & Winston.

Lunzer, E. and Gardner, K. (eds) (1979). *The Effective Use of Reading*, London: Heinemann.

Lunzer, E., Gardner, K., Davies, F. and Greene, T. (1984). *Learning from the Written Word*, Edinburgh: Oliver & Boyd.

Popham, W. J. (1975). *Educational Evaluation*, Englewood Cliffs, NJ: Prentice Hall.

Rosenshine, B. (1983). Teacher functions in instructional programmes, *The Elementary School Journal*, **83** (4), 335–351.

Slavin, R. E. (1983). *Co-operative Learning*, London: Longman.

Thomas, G. (1986). Integrating personnel in order to integrate children, *Support for Learning*, **1** (1), 19–26.

Tomlinson, S. (1982). *A Sociology of Special Education*, London: Routledge & Kegan Paul.

Tyler, R. W. (1949). *Basic Principles of Curriculum and Instruction*, Chicago: University of Chicago Press.

Wheeler, D. K. (1967). *Curriculum Process*, London: University of London Press.

Willmott, A. (1986). The Oxford Certificate of Educational Achievement, in P. Broadfoot (ed.), *Profiles and Records of Achievement*, London: Holt, Rinehart & Winston.

Index